D0537908

((Collins FLAGSHIP HISTORYMAKERS

HITLER

BOOK 1

MARY FULBROOK

((Collins

An imprint of HarperCollins*Publishers*

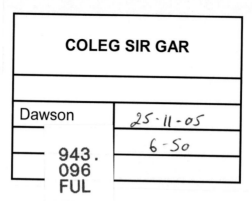

Published by HarperCollins*Publishers* Ltd
77–85 Fulham Palace Road
London
W6 8JB

Browse the complete Collins catalogue at
www.collinseducation.com

© HarperCollins*Publishers* Ltd 2004
First published 2004

ISBN 000 717319 9

Mary Fulbrook asserts the moral right to be
identified as the author of this work.

British Library Cataloguing in Publication Data. A
catalogue record for this book is available from the
British Library.

Series commisioned by Graham Bradbury
Project management by Will Chuter
Edited by Antonia Maxwell
Design by Derek Lee
Picture research by Celia Dearing
Index by Julie Rimington
Production by Sarah Robinson
Printed and bound by Printing Express Ltd.,
Hong Kong

ACKNOWLEDGEMENTS

The Publishers would like to thank the following
for permission to reproduce extracts from their
books:

University of Exeter Press for extracts from *Nazism*,
Jeremy Noakes and Geoffrey Pridham (eds), Exeter
Studies in History, 1983–1998.

The Publishers would like to thank the following
for permission to reproduce pictures on these pages
(T=Top, B=Bottom, L=Left, R=Right, C=Centre):

Akg Images-London 7, 21t, 48; Millions Stand
Behind Me, litho by John Heartfield, 1932, the
Bridgeman Art Library, London/ © The Heartfield
Community of Heirs/VG Bild-Kunst, Bonn and
DACS, London 2004 23; © Corbis 39b, 45, ©
Bettmann/Corbis 13, 39t, 42, 43, 59, © Hulton-
Deutsch Collection/Corbis 19, 29, 58;
Popperfoto.com 21b, 22, 26.

Cover picture: © Bettman/Corbis

Every effort has been made to contact the holders
of copyright material, but if any have been
inadvertently overlooked the Publishers will be
pleased to make the necessary arrangements at the
first opportunity.

Contents

Why do historians differ?

THE purpose of the Flagship Historymakers series is to explore the main debates surrounding a number of key individuals in British, European and American History.

Each book begins with a chronology of the significant events in the life of the individual, and an outline of their career. The book then examines in greater detail three of the most important and controversial issues in the life of the individual – issues which continue to attract differing views from historians, and which feature prominently in examination syllabuses in A-level History and beyond.

Each of these issue sections provides students with an overview of the main arguments put forward by historians. By posing key questions, these sections aim to help students to think through the areas of debate and to form their own judgements on the evidence. It is important, therefore, for students to understand why historians differ in their views on past events and, in particular, on the role of individuals in past events.

The study of history is an ongoing debate about events in the past. Although factual evidence is the essential ingredient of history, it is the *interpretation* of factual evidence that forms the basis for historical debate. The study of how and why historians differ in their various interpretations is termed 'historiography'.

Historical debate can occur for a wide variety of reasons.

Insufficient evidence

In some cases there is insufficient evidence to provide a definitive conclusion. In attempting to 'fill the gaps' where factual evidence is unavailable, historians use their professional judgement to make 'informed comments' about the past.

Availability of evidence

An important reason is the availability of evidence on which to base historical judgements. As new evidence comes to light, an historian today may have more information on which to base judgements than historians in the past. For instance, a major source of information about Nazi Germany are the diaries and reminiscences of Nazi leaders. The diaries of Josef Goebbels were published, in English, in the 1980s. Therefore, it is only relatively recently that historians have been able to analyse and assess this evidence.

A 'philosophy' of history?

Many historians have a specific view of history that will affect the way they make their historical judgements. For instance, Marxist historians – who take their view from the writings of Karl Marx, the founder of modern socialism – believe that society has been made up of competing economic and social classes. They also place considerable importance on economic reasons in human decision making. Therefore, a Marxist historian would regard Nazism as an extreme form of anti-communism. It would be regarded as an anti-modern, anti-progressive movement. This would be a completely different viewpoint to a non-Marxist historian.

The role of the individual

Some historians have seen history as being moulded by the acts of specific individuals. Hitler, Mussolini and Stalin would be seen as individuals who completely changed the course of 20th-century European history. Other historians have tended to 'downplay' the role of individuals; instead, they highlight the importance of more general social, economic and political change. Rather than seeing Adolf Hitler as an individual who changed the course of political history, these historians tend to see him as representing the views of a broader group of individuals: conservative, nationalist, anti-semitic and anti-communist forces in inter-war Germany. Had Hitler not existed, another leader – perhaps Gregor Strasser or Goering – would have taken his place.

Placing different emphasis on the same historical evidence

Even if historians do not possess different philosophies of history or place different emphasis on the role of the individual, it is still possible for them to disagree in one very important way. This is that they may place different emphases on aspects of the same factual evidence. As a result, History should be seen as a subject that encourages debate about the past, based on historical evidence.

Historians will always differ

Historical debate is, in its nature, continuous. What today may be an accepted view about a past event may well change in the future, as the debate continues.

Timeline: Hitler's life

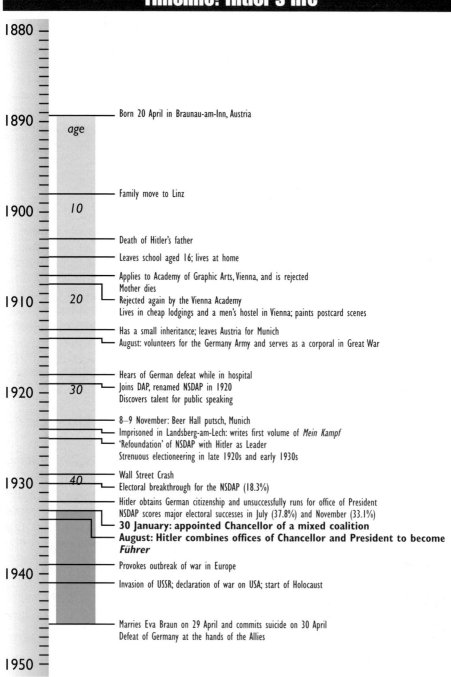

Year	age	Event
1880		
1890		Born 20 April in Braunau-am-Inn, Austria
1900	10	Family move to Linz
		Death of Hitler's father
		Leaves school aged 16; lives at home
		Applies to Academy of Graphic Arts, Vienna, and is rejected
		Mother dies
1910	20	Rejected again by the Vienna Academy
		Lives in cheap lodgings and a men's hostel in Vienna; paints postcard scenes
		Has a small inheritance; leaves Austria for Munich
		August: volunteers for the Germany Army and serves as a corporal in Great War
		Hears of German defeat while in hospital
1920	30	Joins DAP, renamed NSDAP in 1920
		Discovers talent for public speaking
		8–9 November: Beer Hall putsch, Munich
		Imprisoned in Landsberg-am-Lech: writes first volume of *Mein Kampf*
		'Refoundation' of NSDAP with Hitler as Leader
		Strenuous electioneering in late 1920s and early 1930s
1930	40	Wall Street Crash
		Electoral breakthrough for the NSDAP (18.3%)
		Hitler obtains German citizenship and unsuccessfully runs for office of President
		NSDAP scores major electoral successes in July (37.8%) and November (33.1%)
		30 January: appointed Chancellor of a mixed coalition
		August: Hitler combines offices of Chancellor and President to become Führer
1940		Provokes outbreak of war in Europe
		Invasion of USSR; declaration of war on USA; start of Holocaust
		Marries Eva Braun on 29 April and commits suicide on 30 April
		Defeat of Germany at the hands of the Allies
1950		

Hitler in Nazi Party uniform, 1933.

Hitler: a brief biography

How did he make history?

Hitler is one of the most notorious individuals in modern history. Without Hitler, the Holocaust – the organised mass murder of around six million people on grounds of alleged 'racial inferiority' – would not have taken place. Nor, possibly, might the Second World War, which caused the deaths of around 55 million people, and brought unspeakable misery to millions more. The long-term consequences of Hitler's rule were enormous. Military defeat of Germany at the hands of the two new super-powers, the USA and the USSR, brought about the division of Europe in a new Cold War which dominated world affairs for the latter half of the 20th century. The importance of Hitler for understanding 20th-century European and world history cannot be over-estimated.

Or can it? Some historians would argue that Hitler's own personality, his oratorical powers and alleged 'charisma', have been grossly overstated. Was this nondescript upstart, this lower-middle-class Austrian and failed art student, really just the beneficiary of wider forces sweeping Europe in the first half of the 20th century? Were not the economic and political crises in the 'age of extremes' really to blame for the rise of dictators of both left and right – Mussolini in Italy, Stalin in the Soviet Union, as well as Hitler in Germany? And was there not much in Germany's own longer-term history – peculiarities in culture, in 'belated' unification, in rapid and lop-sided political and economic modernisation – which might be just as important in explaining the **Third Reich**? Once in power, was Hitler really the 'strong dictator' depicted in propaganda? And after the collapse of Nazism, has not too much blame been directed at Hitler himself, conveniently (for many contemporaries) over-looking the roles of wider groups in German society? Controversies over the role of Hitler continue to rage furiously.

Third Reich: The 'Third Empire' (1933–45), following the (medieval and early modern) Holy Roman Empire of the German Nation and the (second) German Empire of 1871–1918.

Hitler's early years

Adolf Hitler was born the son of a minor Austrian customs official in the border town of Braunau-am-Inn on 20 April 1889. Although there has been speculation about possible Jewish ancestry, it is most likely that the murky illegitimate roots of Adolf Hitler's father – who was originally baptised Alois Schicklgruber and changed his surname in 1876 – concealed little more than some minor family scandal, possibly involving a degree of incest. Adolf Hitler was the fourth of six children of Alois' marriage to Klara Pölzl. Only one sister, Paula (1896–1960), survived to adulthood; there was also a half-sister and half-brother from one of his father's previous two marriages.

Hitler appears to have had a relatively happy childhood. But, after the family moved to Linz, Hitler's home life was increasingly overshadowed by rows with his overbearing father, for which his mother tried to compensate by showering Hitler with affection. Hitler's father died suddenly in January 1903, when Hitler was 13. As a teenager, Hitler had difficulty making relationships, and performed badly at his secondary school; he was eventually forced to leave and move to another school in Steyr, living in lodgings fifty miles from home. In 1905, at the age of 16, Hitler left school with neither qualifications nor clear plans for the future.

Drifter without aim

In the following years, Hitler drifted, idling for a couple of years at home, nurturing grand plans for a future in art and architecture. Then, at the age of 18 in 1907 he applied unsuccessfully to the Academy of Graphic Arts in Vienna. He suffered a further shattering blow with his mother's death from breast cancer at the age of 47 in December 1907. She seems to have been the one person with whom Hitler was able to form a genuinely close emotional bond. Following renewed failure to enter the Academy in 1908, Hitler lived the life of a respectable down-and-out, indulging his enthusiasm for the opera (particularly Wagner), and living austerely in cheap lodgings and, for a while, in a men's hostel. His position improved with financial help from his aunt, and additional modest earnings painting postcards of Vienna.

Habsburg Empire: The large multi-national Empire of Austria-Hungary (since 1867), ruled by the Austrian Habsburg family. It included not only the German-speaking lands of Austria, but also Hungarians, Serbs, Croats, Slovaks, Romanians, Czechs, Slovenes, Italians and Poles.

During his time in Vienna, Hitler was influenced by widely prevalent anti-Semitic and nationalist ideas, and railed against the cosmopolitan character of the **Habsburg Empire**. He greatly admired Vienna's anti-Semitic mayor, Karl Lueger; but Hitler's own political 'activities' were limited to holding forth to a captive audience in the men's hostel. Hitler also had a couple of Jewish associates who helped him sell his pictures; and indeed, his mother's own doctor, whom Hitler thanked for tending her in her last illness, had been Jewish.

In 1913, aged 24, Hitler finally received his share of his father's inheritance. Having evaded military service in the hated Austrian army since 1909, Hitler took the opportunity to leave Austria for Munich. Tracked down by the Austrian authorities, after years of drifting, he was found unfit for military service. Yet in August 1914, when war was declared, in a fit of enthusiasm Hitler volunteered and was joined up – through bureaucratic oversight – in a Bavarian regiment of the German army.

The making of a politician

The First World War and its aftermath proved the making of Hitler. He enjoyed the camaraderie of the trenches, and the role he held as dispatch runner to the front; he received the Iron Cross twice for bravery, though he was not thought to show 'leadership potential' and was not promoted. His earlier prejudices took firmer shape; when he heard of the end of hostilities in November 1918, while in hospital recovering from a mustard gas attack, he was firmly convinced that 'Jews' and **Bolsheviks** were to blame for a 'stab in the back' causing Germany's defeat.

In 1919–20, Hitler remained as long as possible in Army employment as a 'political education officer'. He discovered that he possessed some talent for public speaking, and was able to stir the emotions of like-minded audiences. Having in the course of his army duties joined the German Workers' Party (**DAP**), a small *völkisch* (right-wing nationalist) party led by Anton Drexler, Hitler rapidly emerged as a leading figure in the renamed National Socialist German Workers' Party (**NSDAP**).

Following the NSDAP's abortive Munich **Beer Hall Putsch** of November 1923 – one of many such uprisings at this turbulent time – Hitler made a propaganda success of the trial. A sympathetic judge pronounced a remarkably lenient sentence. In Landsberg prison, Hitler dictated the first volume of *Mein Kampf*, a rambling and self-serving diatribe full of anti-Semitic prejudices. He was released early, in time for Christmas 1924.

The rise to power

In Hitler's absence, the Nazi movement had splintered. On returning to active politics in 1925 with the 'refoundation' of the NSDAP, Hitler alone proved able to unite the different factions of the party. Now the 'leadership principle' emerged: Hitler himself, as Leader, now embodied the Nazi Movement; there were to be no further debates about the party's Programme.

The key points of Hitler's world view were by now clear: hatred of Jews and **Marxists**, including **Social Democrats**; racial ideology and **social Darwinism**; critique of the evils of modern capitalism, from big department stores and international finance to **cultural decadence**

Bolsheviks: Originally the name for the Communist Party which led the Russian Revolution of October 1917, the term was generalised by the Nazis to apply not only to Communists but even to moderate socialists.

DAP: *Deutsche Arbeiterpartei* (German Workers' Party)

NSDAP: *Nationalsozialistische Deutsche Arbeiterpartei* (National Socialist German Workers' Party)

Beer Hall Putsch: The Nazis' attempt, starting from Munich, to march on Berlin and take over the national government.

Marxists: Technically, followers of the revolutionary ideas of Karl Marx, but the term was greatly over-generalised by the Nazis.

Social Democrats: Moderate socialists committed to reform by democratic means.

Social Darwinism: The application of Charles Darwin's evolutionary theories, including the notion of 'natural selection' and the 'survival of the fittest', to society.

Cultural decadence: A sense that aspects of modern culture were characterised by immorality and the decay of traditional values.

Understanding Hitler

- The son of a minor Austrian customs official, Hitler seemed to speak for the 'little man' and the masses.

- Ill-educated and not an original thinker, Hitler acquired enough 'knowledge' to bolster his prejudices.

- Hitler was fascinated by the visual enactment of power, from the vague art plans of his boyhood, through the political ceremonies, parades and propaganda of the Nazi state, to grandiose architectural dreams for the future face of the Thousand-year Reich.

- Awkward in smaller circles, Hitler was a gifted speaker in large, well-organised settings with a receptive audience.

- Hitler's alleged 'charisma' was as much a matter of the economic and political circumstances as it was of his own personal attributes.

- Hitler was more concerned with his long-term racial and foreign policy goals than with the day-to-day details of policy.

- Hitler's work habits were highly disorganised. He tended to get up late and had little interest in paperwork or the organised practices of 'normal' bureaucratic government.

- Hitler preferred to set the tone and the ultimate goals, and let his subordinates 'fight it out' among themselves.

- Essentially a moody person, Hitler was also given to using controlled outbursts of temper to achieve what he wanted.

- Hitler was an opportunist who turned circumstances to his own advantage; he was also very often simply lucky.

- Hitler, a teetotaller who first became a vegetarian for health reasons in 1924, cultivated an image of kindness to children and animals.

- Hitler was totally without moral scruples, using violence and murder whenever it suited him.

'Hitler is … the purest embodiment of a National Socialist Germany'
Nazi supporter
'Nothing more than a lance-corporal: a conceited braggart'
Fränkische Tagespost, 24 October 1932

(all allegedly 'Jewish'); demands for revision of the harsh 1919 Treaty of Versailles (see p.17), and for territorial expansion to acquire more *Lebensraum* ('living space') for Germans.

As the Depression deepened after the Wall Street Crash of 1929, Hitler's message began to spread. The apparent youth and dynamism of the Nazi movement, with its claims to be a 'party of the people', attracted many voters in a time of crisis. The NSDAP achieved its first electoral breakthrough in 1930; and in 1932, a year of acute political instability, it became the largest party in the Reichstag (German parliament), though its fortunes declined in the autumn. It was in the same year that Hitler (unsuccessfully seeking election as President) finally acquired German citizenship. But it was due to a complex combination of factors that, at the age of 43 in January 1933, Adolf Hitler, despised as the upstart 'Bohemian corporal', was constitutionally appointed Chancellor of Germany by the ageing President Paul von Hindenburg.

Hitler as *Führer*

Once in office, Hitler rapidly destroyed what remained of Weimar democracy. With the death of President Hindenburg in 1934, Hitler combined the offices of Chancellor and President to become absolute *Führer* (or charismatic 'Leader'), thus combining formal ceremonial and political power with a demagogic appeal to the masses.

Hitler's obsessions were put into immediate effect, with discrimination against Jews and the 'hereditarily diseased' and brutal persecution of political opponents. In the mid-1930s, the return to full employment, a degree of consumer satisfaction, and certain peaceful foreign policy successes brought considerable popular support for Hitler, who also fostered his image as charismatic *Führer*. But Hitler's power was inherently unstable.

Blitzkrieg: 'Lightning war' with spectacularly quick military successes.

Even in the first two years of the war, with military successes across Europe in the ***Blitzkrieg***, Hitler retained some popularity. It was only in 1941, with the invasion of the USSR and declaration of war on the USA, that the tide began to turn. Hitler's dual goals of racial 'cleansing', culminating in mass genocide, and military 'world mastery', culminating in world war, were ultimately to prove fatal for Hitler himself as well as for the millions whose deaths he had caused.

Hitler had little by way of a private life outside politics. He had been a loner in Vienna and even among comrades in the trenches of the Great War, although he developed intense relationships with

Eva Braun (1910–45): Hitler's long-term female companion.

close political associates later on. A brief entanglement with his half-niece, Angela ('Geli') Raubel, ended in her suicide at the age of 23 in 1931; subsequently Hitler developed a liaison with **Eva Braun**. Always a hypochondriac, Hitler increasingly took medications which exacerbated his stormy moods, causing him to withdraw ever more from public life. As his dream of a 'Thousand-year Reich' lay shattered and Russian troops moved into the ruins of Berlin, Hitler despaired. On 29 April 1945, in his underground bunker, Hitler married Eva Braun; on 30 April, alongside Eva Braun, at the age of 56 Adolf Hitler committed suicide.

Hitler's Bavarian mountain retreat, the Berghof on the Obersalzburg near Berchtesgaden.

How did Hitler ever become Chancellor of Germany?

Was Weimar democracy 'doomed from the start'?

How important were attacks on the system by elites?

How did the Nazis achieve political breakthrough?

Framework of events

1918	9 November: Emperor resigns, Republic is declared; 11 November: Armistice
1919	Weimar Constitution, Treaty of Versailles.
	Hitler joins DAP
1920	DAP renamed NSDAP. 25-point Party 'Programme' announced
1923	French and Belgian troops occupy the Ruhr
	Great inflation
	8–9 November: Beer Hall Putsch, Munich
1924	Hitler imprisoned in Landsberg-am-Lech, released by Christmas
1925	'Refoundation' of the NSDAP
	Death of President Ebert, replaced by Hindenburg
1928	Müller cabinet. NSDAP scores 2.6% of vote (12 deputies) in General Election
1929	Wall Street crash.
	Referendum on Young Plan
1930	Müller replaced by Brüning as Chancellor
	September elections: NSDAP scores 18.3%, 107 deputies
1932	Brüning replaced by von Papen
	Elections of 31 July: NSDAP polls 37.8% of vote, 230 deputies
	Elections of 6 November: NSDAP polls 33.1% of vote, 196 deputies
	Von Papen replaced by von Schleicher as Chancellor
1933	30 January: Hindenburg appoints Hitler Chancellor of a mixed cabinet
	27 February: Reichstag fire
	5 March elections: NSDAP polls 43.9% of vote

GIVEN the appalling consequences, the arguments about who or what was responsible for Hitler's rise to power range over an immensely wide terrain. Historical controversies range from detailed empirical questions – such as which social groups voted for the NSDAP, or what was the role of big business in financing Hitler – to much wider interpretations of the period as a whole.

Some historians emphasise long-term peculiarities of German history, appealing to notions of a *Sonderweg* ('special path') to modernity; others point to features common to many European states after the First World War. For some, the problem has to do with 'modern mass society' and hence Nazism is an instance of **totalitarianism**; for others, adopting a Marxist approach, Nazism has to do with 'crises of capitalism' and is hence a variant of **fascism**. And some concentrate primarily on one individual: Hitler. Hitler's personal power has been emphasised – indeed over-emphasised – in many popular biographies and films, as well as historical works, as though Hitler's 'spell' had been something people could not resist. Even among those historians focusing on the same period, there are often huge differences of emphasis in choosing where precisely to lay the blame.

It is possible to simplify this complex story somewhat by analysing two separate but closely interrelated developments. One was the instability and eventual destruction of democracy in Weimar Germany. The other was the rise of a mass party under Hitler's leadership. It was when the political and economic crises came to a head that the combination proved fatal. Those individuals who played a key role in destroying democracy were unable to find a stable solution on their own; they thought that in 'taming' Hitler, they could harness the power of the masses to the purposes of the elites. This final gamble proved tragically flawed.

Thus Hitler benefited from much wider historical currents. Only in very specific circumstances was this Austrian drifter able eventually to gain a position of power in the German state, from which he could go on to shape European and world history.

Totalitarianism: This term has been defined in a variety of ways: it generally refers to a streamlined state with one leader, one party and one ideology, based on repression and indoctrination, and it emphasises the similarities between dictatorships of the Right (Hitler's Nazism, Mussolini's Fascism) and the Left (Stalin's Communism).

Fascism: Originally referring to Mussolini's Italy, this concept has been generalised by some historians to encompass modern right-wing dictatorships, including Nazism.

Was Weimar democracy 'doomed from the start'?

The legacies of the First World War

As Ian Kershaw has aptly written, the First World War 'made Hitler possible'. The experience and aftermath of war shaped Hitler's outlook and gave him the opportunity to enter post-war German politics; at the same time it created an audience receptive to his prejudices. Kershaw continues: 'Without the war, a Hitler on the Chancellor's seat that had been occupied by Bismarck would have been unthinkable' (Kershaw, *Hitler 1889–1936: Hubris*, p.73).

Landmark Study   **The book that changed people's views**

Ian Kershaw, *Hitler 1889–1936: Hubris* (Penguin, 1998) and *Hitler 1936–1945: Nemesis* (Penguin, 2000)

Ian Kershaw's masterly two-volume biography of Adolf Hitler is unrivalled. Kershaw combines extensive archival research with original insights to produce an outstanding analysis of Hitler's development and historical role. This biography is notable not merely for recreating minute details of Hitler's life in a wider historical context, but also for the fundamental contribution it makes to central historical controversies. Kershaw succeeds in combining a central focus on the personality and ideas of Hitler with a complex analysis of the chaotic structures and processes of decision-making in the Third Reich. His concept of 'working towards the Führer' provides a way through the controversy between 'functionalists' and 'intentionalists'. Volume One is essential to understanding the rise of Hitler.

'Working towards the Führer': A phrase used by contemporaries: carrying out Hitler's assumed will without being given an explicit order.

Functionalists: Historians who emphasise the consequences of the ways in which the increasingly chaotic structures of power in Nazi Germany functioned.

Intentionalists: Historians who emphasise the importance of Hitler's intentions as the key cause of developments in Nazi Germany.

But – as Kershaw also reminds us – making 'Hitler possible' does not mean making Hitler inevitable. How important, then, was the war in explaining the collapse of Weimar democracy?

The psychological and social consequences of the 'Great War' of 1914–18 were undoubtedly of massive significance. The experience of 'total war' involved not merely soldiers but also civilians on the home front: women and young people participated in economic production, and in food riots and strikes. For some soldiers at the front, the experience of the mud-filled trenches, the daily witnessing of the maiming and deaths of comrades in stalemate battles over a few yards of territory, aroused a hatred of war itself. For others – like Hitler – it fed into rabid hatred of the culprits allegedly responsible for German defeat, the 'Jews' and 'Bolsheviks', and a determination to take revenge. This 'stab in the back' myth proved to be of major importance in the turmoil and upheavals of the post-war years. So too, in very different ways, did the shell-shock, the sense of disorientation, and the difficulties of reintegration into civil society following demobilisation. The immediate post-war years were characterised by widespread hunger and high death rates from diseases such as influenza, as well as rioting, strikes, political instability and violence. Many people in this devastated post-war society – with its high numbers of war widows, orphans, teenagers without fathers or elder brothers – had a totally unrealistic set of expectations about what the new Republic could offer, as Richard Bessel has shown (*Germany after the First World War,* 1993).

In this wider context, the harsh terms of the **Versailles Treaty** of 1919 caused massive resentment. Loss of colonies abroad and territory at home, the ban on an air force, restrictions on the size of the army and navy, and demilitarisation of border areas, were heavy blows, as was the infamous 'War Guilt clause' laying primary blame for unleashing the war on Germany and her allies. Weimar was born

Versailles Treaty, 1919

Territorial changes:

- Loss of colonies abroad
- Alsace-Lorraine to be returned to France
- France to benefit from the coal production of the Saar
- West Prussia, Upper Silesia and Posen to go to a reconstituted state of Poland
- Danzig to become a free city under the supervision of the new League of Nations
- Demilitarisation of Germany's border areas
- Left bank of the Rhine to be under Allied supervision for 15 years

Restrictions on power:

- No union of Germany and Austria permitted
- German Army to be reduced to 100 000 men, for domestic and border-guard duties only
- Restrictions on German Navy, and submarines forbidden
- No German Air Force permitted

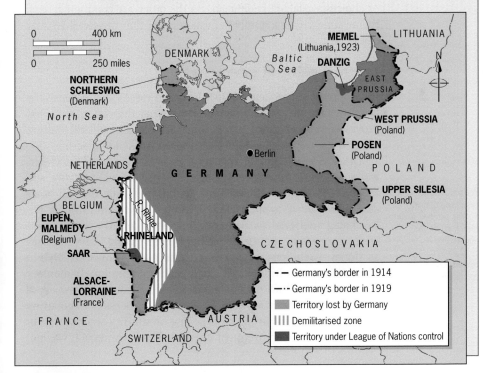

of a humiliating defeat, and the nationalist resentment caused by the Versailles Treaty could readily be exploited as a binding force across different social groups who would otherwise have had little in common.

Reparations: Payments to make good some of the losses caused by the war.

Reparations, when the extent was revealed in 1920, also proved to be a long-running source of discontent. However, there is controversy over precisely why reparations were such a liability. For a long time it was held that the absolute level of reparations was indeed a major economic millstone, rendering Weimar capitalism intrinsically weak. More recently, as Theo Balderston outlines (*Economics and Politics in the Weimar Republic,* 2002), historians have argued that the major problems were the ways in which reparations were perceived and presented, in terms of Germany's 'capacity to pay' (or not), and the ways in which politicians chose to deal with reparations. Inflation, already rooted in the financing of the war through bonds rather than taxes, was made very much worse by the government's decision simply to print more and more paper money, leading to the massive inflation of 1923. Whatever the balance of these debates, the reparations issue dogged Weimar's brief life.

More generally, the balance between structural economic and political weaknesses on the one hand, and the 'freedom of manoeuvre' or choices available to politicians on the other, are common general themes underlying a number of debates over the collapse of Weimar democracy.

Intrinsic political weaknesses?

It has often been argued that further weaknesses were rooted in the constitution and political system. On further inspection, this view proves somewhat problematic, since aspects of political culture affected the way in which the constitution worked in practice.

The Weimar Republic appeared to be immensely democratic: women as well as men over the age of 20 had the right to vote; and the system of **proportional representation** meant that all votes cast were given appropriately weighted representation in the Reichstag (national parliament). Yet, in a country where there were numerous political parties representing very narrow sectional – religious, regional or social class – interests, this in effect led to a multiplicity of small parties gaining parliamentary representation. With no single party able to acquire a majority of seats on its own, parties were in a constant process of negotiating unstable coalitions on the basis of one or another shaky compromise, and there were frequent changes of government. It was not

Proportional representation: A voting system in which political parties gain representation in parliament according to the percentage of votes that they receive.

necessarily the system of proportional representation as such that was the problem therefore, but rather the character of Weimar parties under particular social and economic circumstances.

The role of the President of the Weimar Republic:
● Elected directly by the people, to serve for a seven-year term
● Has power to appoint and dismiss Chancellors
● Article 48: power to rule by emergency decree

The **role of the President**, who was voted in for seven years by direct popular vote, was often said to be that of an *Ersatz Kaiser*: a 'substitute Emperor', with considerable personal powers. In particular, the President's powers to appoint and dismiss Chancellors, and to rule by emergency decree under the notorious Article 48, have been the subject of much critique. But such powers could be used to stabilise, as well as to undermine, democracy: it was not Article 48 itself, which was used by Weimar's first President and committed democrat, Friedrich Ebert, to stabilise the Republic, but rather its later misuse by President Hindenburg to undermine democracy, which proved problematic.

Flawed revolution and fatal compromises?

Weimar Republic:
The Republic was named after the town of Weimar in which its first parliament met, because of the continuing political unrest in Berlin at the time.

The birth of the **Weimar Republic** – a result of sailors' and soldiers' mutinies and massive revolutionary unrest, causing the flight of the Emperor and the ad hoc declaration of a Republic – was accompanied by a series of compromises which dogged its brief life.

One such compromise was the agreement made between the civilian government under **Friedrich Ebert**, and the Army under General Groener, in November 1918. Ebert's pact with the Army has been criticised as unnecessary, allowing the old regime to retain its power and regroup; it has been defended as essential to orderly demobilisation and maintaining order in a time of crisis. The result was that the Army continued to play a powerful role in politics, which was eventually to prove fatal in undermining democracy. It also played a role in unleashing bitter splits among the left. Along with the so-called 'Free Corps' units, the Army was involved in suppression of popular unrest, particularly that of a left-wing persuasion. The murder of the Spartacist (left-wing communist) leaders Karl

Friedrich Ebert (1871–1925)
Of relatively humble background, Ebert joined the SPD in 1889; as a trade union activist, he was on the police 'black list'; he held assorted jobs, until elected to the Reichstag in 1912; and became joint leader of the SPD in 1913. Nominated first Chancellor of the newly declared Weimar Republic on the Kaiser's abdication on 9 November 1918, Ebert oversaw the armistice and the difficult transition to parliamentary democracy. He became Weimar's first President in August 1919, and used Article 48 to stabilise Weimar democracy. Ebert was criticised by the left for using the Army and Free Corps units to suppress workers' uprisings, and for failing to engage in a radical revolution; he was criticised by the right for his support of trade unions and workers' rights. Died prematurely from appendicitis in 1925.

Liebknecht and Rosa Luxemburg in January 1919 led to lasting hostility between Social Democrats and Communists, making co-operation against Nazism much more problematic a decade later.

Another key compromise was that between the employers' organisations and the trade unions, in the Stinnes-Legien agreement of November 1918. This gave trade unions formal recognition and rights which, in employers' eyes, were fundamentally linked to the democratic system as such. Although the institutional framework was partially dismantled within a matter of years, and the resources and strength of trade unions declined massively with widespread unemployment after 1929, this too would prove to be a highly problematic legacy in discrediting democracy in the eyes of many leading industrialists.

Ebert has been further criticised for failing to engage in full-scale social revolution, resting content with a mere political revolution, leaving the power of the old elites intact. A committed democrat, Ebert felt people should be able to make their preferences known through the ballot box. In the event, the ballot box proved indecisive, the early 'Weimar coalition' of moderate parties led by the SPD lasting little over a year.

On both the left and the right, massive discontent continued. There were repeated attempts to take political control by violence, from the left-wing uprisings in Munich in 1919 and in Thuringia and Saxony in 1923, to the rightwing Kapp Putsch of 1920 and the Nazi 'Beer Hall Putsch' of 1923. Amidst continued violence on the streets, there were frequent political assassinations, including that of the Foreign Minister Walter Rathenau in 1922.

Was there the potential for stabilisation?

For all these undoubted weaknesses, the 'doomed from the start' school of historians have not clinched their case. Hitler's first unsuccessful attempt at seizure of power, in November 1923, was in the very year in which Weimar democracy suffered its worst early crises, with the French and Belgian occupation of the Ruhr, and massive inflation spiralling out of control. Hitler's miserable attempt to emulate Mussolini's successful march on Rome ended as a damp squib, the hoped-for 'march on Berlin' stopped dead in its tracks, still in the centre of Munich within hours of its muddled launch. Despite a successful propaganda stand by Hitler at his trial, which received national publicity, by 1924 the early troubles of the Weimar Republic seemed effectively over, the chances of a Hitler ever becoming German Chancellor effectively nil.

Munich Putsch,
8–9 November 1923.
A special unit of
Putschists.

In the middle years of the 1920s, with inflation under control, reparations repayments renegotiated under the Dawes Plan of 1924, and considerable foreign policy successes under the long-serving Foreign Minister, **Gustav Stresemann** – known as a *Vernunft-republikaner* ('Republican of conviction') – the Weimar Republic looked set for long-term stabilisation (for a recent evaluation, see Jonathan Wright, *Gustav Stresemann*, 2002). Historians dispute the extent of 'stabilisation' in Weimar's middle years, which were not entirely the 'golden twenties' they are sometimes portrayed as being; but war-time legacies, new political structures and the general turbulence of the early years do not, on their own, amount to a sufficient explanation of Weimar's eventual collapse a decade later.

**Gustav Stresemann
(1878–1929)**

Elected to the Reichstag in 1907; became leader of the National Liberal Party in 1917. Formed the German People's Party (DVP) in 1918. As Chancellor of a coalition government from 13 August to 23 November 1923, Stresemann successfully resolved the major crises of that year (French occupation of the Ruhr, massive inflation).

From 1924 until his untimely death from a stroke in 1929, Stresemann served as Foreign Minister. Although initially an authoritarian and supporter of the use of military force, Stresemann became convinced of the need to support the Republic and to find peaceful solutions to Germany's problems; the renegotiation of reparations

in the Dawes Plan (1924) and Young Plan (1929), and the diplomatic achievements of the Locarno Pact (1925), the Treaty of Berlin (1926) and Germany's admission to the League of Nations (1926), were key elements in the potential stabilisation of Weimar democracy.

How important were attacks on the system by elites?

President Paul von Hindenburg (1847–1934)
A military man — who had fought already in the Austro-Prussian War of 1866 and the Franco-Prussian War of 1870 — Hindenburg was brought out of retirement to serve in the First World War. Having scored a notable victory at the battle of Tannenberg in 1914, Hindenburg went on to play a prominent role in the war, as Field Marshal and then Army Chief of Staff. Widely popular as a military hero, despite his advanced age Hindenburg was elected President on Ebert's death in 1925, and narrowly re-elected on a second ballot in 1932. By the time he appointed Hitler Chancellor in 1933 — a mere 18 months before his own death — he was already suffering from senility.

Coalition government: A government made up of more than one party, in coalitions which, during the Weimar period, were generally very unstable.

The various weaknesses and ambiguous legacies of Weimar's difficult birth need not inevitably have caused serious problems. It was rather the ways in which they were represented (in the case of German defeat) or dealt with (in the case of reparations) that led to the real problems. Such perceptions and choices were, moreover, rooted in a wider problem: that of a lack of widespread support for democracy in principle.

The real problem of Weimar was, it is sometimes suggested, that it was a 'Republic without Republicans'. The right criticised Weimar for being an ineffective parliamentary democracy tainted by dishonourable defeat and by forms of cultural modernism; and on the left, socialists were critical of the ills of capitalism, while Communists were not committed to the democratic political system either. Thus a highly divided polit-ical culture was a key ingredient in Weimar's fragility. But we have to be very clear about where precisely to lay the blame for bringing democracy down.

The roles of key elites

Weimar democracy was ironically itself arguably a victim of a 'stab in the back' – and this precisely by those most important individuals and groups who should have shouldered the responsibility of upholding the political system.

The 'revolution' of 1918 was only a partial one. Many of the traditional elites – the civil service, the judiciary, the Army, teachers in universities and schools, business elites – were far from enthusiastic about the new political system, and harked back to the 'good old days' of Imperial Germany. Thus, for example, the lenient sentences meted out by judges to those found guilty of political crimes on the right contrasted strongly with the very harsh sentences given to those found guilty of similar offences on the left. The frequent changes of **coalition government** gave rise to widespread criticisms of the 'system' with its party squabbling; many thought that the real problem was the 'emergence of the masses' in a democracy, and that the old authoritarian political system had been a great deal more effective.

President Paul von Hindenburg, a military hero from the Great War, replaced Weimar's first president, Friedrich Ebert, when the latter died prematurely from appendicitis in 1925. Although consti-tutionally empowered to uphold the Republic, **Hindenburg** from the very start yearned for a more autocratic form of government. Hindenburg's use of presidential rule under Article 48 from 1930 onwards effectively brought democracy to an end well before he made the final mistake of appointing Hitler to the Chancellorship. The Army leadership, too, under General von Von Schleicher from 1926, held anti-democratic views, and was deeply committed to revision of Treaty of Versailles. Von Schleicher was to become particularly important in the political machinations of 1932–3.

Economic elites were not on the whole convinced democrats either, associating democracy with increased power and voice for workers and trade unions. Many agrarian elites – particularly the landowners who in Prussia, known as *Junkers,* had long held a dominant political position – were severely hit by an agrarian crisis in the 1920s, which set in well before the Wall Street Crash; they also generally favoured a return to authoritarian government along the lines of Imperial Germany.

The role of big business in the rise of Hitler has been a particular focus of historical controversy. According to the orthodox Marxist interpretation, Nazism was a variant of the wider phenomenon of 'fascism', the last ditch of modern capitalism in a period of crisis. The famous John Heartfield poster, showing Hitler with an outstretched hand backwards to receive a wad of money, fed the myth that business tycoons 'paid Hitler'. However, research by Henry Ashby Turner (*German Big Business and the Rise of Hitler*, 1985) and others has revealed a far less simplistic picture.

'The real meaning of the Hitler salute': famous poster by political photomontage artist John Heartfield (1891–1968) of Hitler receiving a backhander.

Many businessmen were against the Weimar system of parliamentary democracy and political parties. They were against Marxism, which, like Hitler, they understood to include Social Democrats and other non-Marxist socialists as well as Bolsheviks; and they were opposed to what they saw as the power of trade unions which appeared to be guaranteed by the system. Most wanted some form of authoritarian government. In all of this, their general aims were compatible with those of Hitler.

However, this did not by any stretch of the imagination make most of them pro-Nazi. Many despised Hitler, who did not fit in well with their social circles;

very few were actually supporters of the NSDAP. The handful of exceptions included the long-time financial supporter and Ruhr steelworks magnate, Fritz Thyssen; the relatively small businessman and organiser of the 'Keppler circle' of economic advisers to Hitler, Wilhelm Keppler; the right-wing President of the Reichsbank Hjalmar Schacht, who finally broke with Hitler's government in 1937; and the Cologne banker Baron Kurt von Schroeder, whose capacity to speak on behalf of the wider business community appears to have been greatly over-estimated.

After the election of 1930, however – when the NSDAP gained a surprising 18.3 per cent of the vote – and in face of the growing political and economic crisis, many businessmen began to hedge their bets. At the same time, Hitler seized the opportunity to woo the business vote, or at least to neutralise potential hostility. He had greatly benefited from association with the conservative press baron Hugenberg (leader of the **DNVP**) in campaigning against the **Young Plan** (to replace the **Dawes Plan** on reparations) in 1929. He remained associated with – though keeping some distance from – the forces of 'national opposition' in the **Harzburg Front** of 11 October 1931, and followed this up with a speech at the Düsseldorf Industry Club on 27 January 1932.

DNVP: The national conservative, and under Hugenberg increasingly right-wing, 'German National People's Party' (*Deutschnationale Volkspartei*).

Young Plan/Dawes Plan: The Dawes Plan of 1924 regularised Germany's reparations payments in the short term and promoted an influx of foreign loans to boost the German economy. The Young Plan of 1929 was designed to be a final settlement of a much-reduced reparations bill, to be paid over a long period (59 years).

Harzburg Front: A loose right-wing grouping resulting from a meeting of nationalist opposition forces in Bad Harzburg, including the DNVP and the veterans' organisation, the *Stahlhelm*.

Many businessmen remained unconvinced by Hitler's (often deliberate) vagueness on economic policies, and continued to greet Nazism with a degree of scepticism. Nevertheless, in 1932, in the context of growing political crisis, attitudes were shifting. A small number of businessmen and bankers handed in a petition to Hindenburg on 19 November 1932, which falsely gave Hindenburg the impression of a far wider basis of support among this community for Hitler. Some key individuals were also involved in the final discussions of late January 1933.

Thus, while business antipathy to 'the system' was an element in the destruction of Weimar democracy, on the whole big business played much less of an active role in levering Hitler into power. Even Hitler's attempted neutralisation of the business community had a price to be paid, since it aroused disquiet among some of his own more radical supporters in the NSDAP. The difficulties of juggling the demands and interests of both radical followers and powerful traditional elites were to become increasingly evident once Hitler was in power.

The two separate strands – the disillusionment of the elites with the system of Weimar democracy, and Hitler's own pursuit of power – were increasingly flowing together. But it took conditions of major crisis for the NSDAP to become a genuinely mass party, and for the old elites to run out of alternative strategies, and to turn in desperation to Hitler.

How did the Nazis achieve political breakthrough?

In 1925, when Hitler returned to political life, the NSDAP was disintegrating into squabbling factions. He soon found a capacity to unite different wings under loyalty to his own person as undisputed Leader. Yet in the relatively stable period of the mid-1920s, the party itself was little more than a tiny drop in the complex ocean of Weimar politics: in the elections of 1928, the NSDAP scored a mere 2.6 per cent of vote, with twelve deputies in the Reichstag. Its staggering rise in the following years can only be explained in terms of the way in which it was able to exploit and benefit from the mounting economic and political crises following the Wall Street Crash of 1929.

Nazi ideology, propaganda, organisation and tactics

Most Weimar political parties appealed to the particularistic interests of different sections of the community, with material interests directly opposed to each other (conservative nationalists versus Communists, for example) or specific religious interests to defend (the Catholic Centre Party). The NSDAP, by contrast, claimed to be a *Volkspartei* ('People's Party'), capable of healing the divisions of modern society and uniting all Germans together in a harmonious 'national community'. Most Weimar parties projected a somewhat dry, dull and bureaucratic image, an image of middle-aged men embroiled in self-serving coalition squabbles. The NSDAP by contrast appeared youthful, dynamic, and vigorous, as well as totally untainted by power and responsibility.

The NSDAP was not even saddled with any very specific policies. Nazi ideology was both grandiose and vague. Vehemently nationalist, Nazis railed against the Treaty of Versailles, the **'November criminals'**, Jews and Bolshevists. On capitalism, the arguments were equally negative: against large department stores which were increasingly threatening the livelihood of small shopkeepers; against 'international finance capital', behind which allegedly lay the hand of 'international Jewry'; against all the cultural evils of 'modern capitalism', including 'decadent' jazz music, the emancipation of women, and 'degenerate' morals. At the same time the Nazis were virulently anti-Communist, and again saw the hands of Jews lurking behind Bolshevism. There was a scapegoat for everything.

'November criminals': Those accused of being responsible for Germany's military defeat in November 1918.

Hitler speaking at a rally of right-wing nationalist groups, including the DNVP, the *Stahlhelm* and the Nazis, in Bad Harzburg on 11 October 1931.

The Nazi message was put across through well-targeted propaganda and clever organisational tactics. An extensive regional system allowed the infiltration and on occasion take-over of social and professional organisations, targeting groups such as small farmers, lawyers, doctors and teachers, women and students. In an age before television, and with slowly increasing but still limited radio ownership, personal appearances and well-orchestrated campaign meetings were of vital importance. Perhaps the first modern politician to make major use of the aeroplane to speak in as many places as possible, Hitler was able to exploit campaign meetings with enormous success, developing his oratorical powers and other tricks for heightening audience expectations.

Who voted for the NSDAP?

Yet without the economic and political crises unleashed by the withdrawal of short-term American loans from the already fragile German economy following the Wall Street Crash of 1929, the NSDAP might still have remained a fringe party. Its growing electoral support in the elections of 1930 and July 1932 was directly related to the growth of mass unemployment, and the growth of political instability, in this period.

The SPD-led Müller coalition cabinet of 1928–30 eventually fell apart over the question of whether to deal with rising unemployment by lowering unemployment benefits, or raising taxes. Müller's successor as Chancellor, Brüning, was unable to command a parliamentary majority. When, in the elections of September

1930, the NSDAP suddenly scored 18.3 per cent of the vote, and a threatening phalanx of 107 Nazi deputies marched into the Reichstag, many parties including the SPD decided it would be better to tolerate the Brüning government rather than risk further elections. Thus from 1930, Weimar democracy was essentially at an end, as Presidential use of Article 48 allowed Brüning to put through unpopular legislation against the wishes of the majority of members of parliament.

Brüning's economic policies have been the subject of massive controversy among historians. Brüning chose to adopt deflationary measures, preferring rising unemployment to other possible strategies for tackling the growing crisis. By 1932, six million people – around one in three of the workforce – were unemployed. Historians (notably Carl-Ludwig Holtfrerich and Knut Borchardt) disagree about the extent to which alternative policies were or were not available to Brüning, or the extent of his 'freedom of manoeuvre' (see Balderston, and Holtfrerich's essay in Ian Kershaw (ed.), *Weimar: Why did German Democracy Fail?*, 1990). But there is no doubt about the consequences: as unemployment rose, so too did support for the Nazis.

This is not because the unemployed voted for the NSDAP. As the research of Thomas Childers (*The Nazi Voter*, 1983) has shown, it was the fear of unemployment, rather than unemployment itself, which tended to make people look to the Nazi party for ways out of

The vote for the Catholic Centre Party (and its Catholic 'sister party', the BVP) remained remarkably constant. It was primarily the parties of the 'bourgeois centre' which catastrophically lost votes to the NSDAP. Had the Social Democrats (SPD) and Communists (KPD) combined forces, they would have presented stronger opposition to the Nazis.

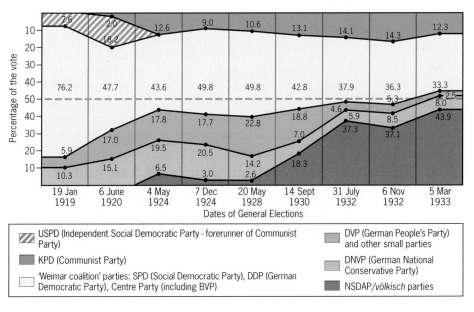

Legend:
USPD (Independent Social Democratic Party - forerunner of Communist Party)

KPD (Communist Party)

'Weimar coalition' parties: SPD (Social Democratic Party), DDP (German Democratic Party), Centre Party (including BVP)

DVP (German People's Party) and other small parties

DNVP (German National Conservative Party)

NSDAP/*völkisch* parties

the crisis. The NSDAP vote was concentrated particularly among the agrarian and small-town lower middle classes, in the predominantly Protestant areas of northern and eastern Germany; in other words, among those who still had something to lose, and who feared loss of social status. Catholics tended to remain loyal to the Catholic Centre party; and the workers who were laid off first, and hence were unemployed, tended to remain loyal to the traditional parties of the working class, the SPD and KPD. The NSDAP appears to have benefited from what Larry Eugene Jones (*German Liberalism and the Dissolution of the Weimar Party System*, 1988) has called the 'collapse of the bourgeois middle'. While never genuinely representing the whole 'national community', the NSDAP nevertheless was able to mobilise a relatively wide cross-section of society in times of crisis. At its peak, it drew not only on the core voters mentioned above, but also garnered significant support among some sections of the working class – particularly those in small enterprises who had not been organised in unions or other workers' movements – and among the middle and professional classes.

The Brüning government fell, not because of increased support for Nazism – there was no further general election during Brüning's Chancellorship – but because Brüning lost the support of President Hindenburg (in part because of Brüning's mismanagement of Hindenburg's campaign to stand again as President when his seven-year term came to an end in 1932). Brüning's successor, Franz von Papen, was totally unable to cobble together any kind of parliamentary support. In the elections of July 1932, following his appointment as Chancellor, his position worsened dramatically: the NSDAP won a staggering 37.8 per cent of the vote – their highest under more or less genuinely democratic conditions, – and, with their 230 deputies in the Reichstag alongside the equally anti-democratic communist bloc, there was an anti-democratic 'wrecking majority' that could block normal parliamentary processes. The government seemed to be caught in deadlock, with Hitler as leader of the largest party.

How did Hitler finally get appointed Chancellor?

Yet Hitler was not offered the Chancellorship in the summer of 1932. The most that Hindenburg could bring himself to offer was the Vice-Chancellorship, a suggestion which Hitler greeted with derision, much to the dismay and anger of many members of his party who felt he had thrown away the best chance they would ever get. Von Papen limped on for a few more months, losing a vote of no confidence in the Reichstag on 12 September by 512 votes to 42.

General von Schleicher (1882–1934)
A military man who played an increasingly important role in the Brüning government and in the intrigues of 1932–3. In his brief stint as Chancellor of Germany (December 1932 – January 1933), Schleicher sought to make an arrangement with the 'left wing' of the NSDAP. He was murdered in the 'Night of the Long Knives' on 30 June 1934.

Nazi fortunes apparently on the wane

During the autumn of 1932, the first signs of economic recovery began to be felt. Meanwhile, the fortunes of the Nazi party appeared to take a turn for the worse, with funds and energy exhausted by the almost constant electioneering of the year. In the elections of 6 November 1932, the Nazi vote declined to 33.1 per cent of the vote, with 196 deputies in the Reichstag. The party itself was split further by the willingness of its more radical wing, in the person of Gregor Strasser, to enter into discussions with the new and short-lived Chancellor, **General von Schleicher**, who had finally taken over government after playing a key role in many of the political machinations of preceding months.

Ironically, it was precisely because Hitler had been losing popular support – while yet remaining leader of the largest party in the Reichstag – and because his party appeared split and weakened, that Hitler no longer appeared quite so much of a threat. Thus, it looked more likely that he could be co-opted and 'tamed' by those who wished to harness his mass following for their own purposes.

Political deadlock: the apparent lack of any stable alternative

Von Schleicher's Chancellorship of a matter of weeks from December 1932 to January 1933 was even more short-lived than that of his predecessor. During this period, he failed to gain the support of trade unionists and the 'left wing' of the NSDAP, and at the same time managed to antagonise industrialists and agrarian elites. By January 1932, there was almost total political deadlock in Germany. Von Schleicher himself had commissioned a report (the 'Ott Report') the previous autumn which claimed to show that the Army could not control the rising levels of political violence on the streets, particularly in the event of civil war.

The final 'backstairs intrigue'

In late January 1933, the fatal combination came together. Elites were not prepared to uphold democracy at any cost; most wanted some form of authoritarian government. Hitler, as leader of the largest party, was insistent on the Chancellorship or nothing. With loss of votes, morale and membership, organisationally split, and suffering heavy debts, the NSDAP no longer seemed so dangerous. In these circumstances, an ageing Hindenburg was persuaded, by a

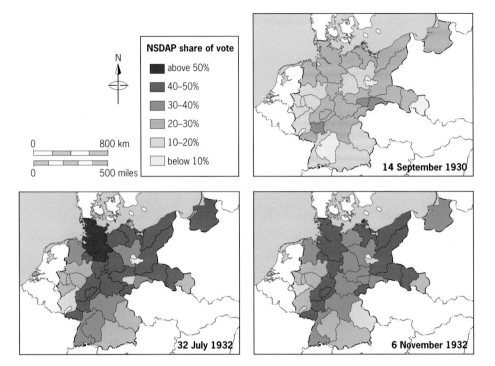

The electoral performance of the NSDAP 1930–33.

SA: The brown-shirted *Sturmabteilung* ('storm troopers'), a paramilitary organisation of the NSDAP.

Reichstag fire: The German parliament building (Reichstag) was set on fire by an arson attack which the Nazis blamed on Communists and used as a pretext for declaring a state of emergency in the run-up to the election.

small group including his own son and von Papen, to appoint Hitler leader of mixed cabinet in which there were only two other Nazis.

On the evening of 30 January 1933, the **SA** celebrated Hitler's appointment as Chancellor with a torch-lit parade through the centre of Berlin; within days, political opponents were being rounded up, brutally beaten and tortured, while Hitler unveiled his megalomaniac plans for the future. Following the **Reichstag fire** of 27 February, under conditions of intimidation and violence, the Nazi party still failed to gain an absolute majority of the vote; in the elections of 5 March 1933, the NSDAP polled just under 44 per cent of the vote. Hitler had been handed power by the old guard, while a majority of the population remained unwilling to support him. It did not take Hitler long to ensure he would no longer need to pay heed to such electoral matters.

The death of Weimar democracy: accident, suicide or murder?

The answer to this question is complex: there was an element of each. 'Accident', because had the Wall Street crash not occurred there would have been some chance for continued stabilisation over time; 'suicide', because key elites had no will to uphold democracy and took the wrong decisions, most tragically at the very end; and 'murder', because Hitler made no secret of his intention to destroy democracy, having abused the democratic system to attain power by constitutional means. On balance, Hitler had a great deal of luck as well as political ability; he was the beneficiary of developments which had taken place for reasons not of his own making.

 How did Hitler ever become Chancellor of Germany?

1. Read the following extract and answer the question.

   'When the speech was over, there was roaring enthusiasm and applause. Hitler saluted, gave his thanks, the Horst Wessel song sounded out … Then he went. – How many look up to him with touching faith! As their helper, their saviour, their deliverer from unbearable distress – to him who rescues the Prussian prince, the scholar, the clergyman, the farmer, the worker, the unemployed, who rescues them from the parties back into the nation.'

   (Eye-witness account of a Hitler election rally in 1932; reprinted in Noakes and Pridham, vol. 1, p. 74.)

   How useful is this source in explaining the rise of popular support for Hitler and the NSDAP?

2. 'From 1924, the Weimar Republic was potentially on the road to stability; it was only the mistakes of key individuals after 1929 which ultimately destroyed democracy in Germany.' How far do you agree with this statement?

How did political structures develop in the process of 'cumulative radicalisation'?

Does Hitler's leadership style provide evidence of strength or weakness?

How far can policies be explained in terms of Hitler's 'programme'?

Framework of events

Phase I: *Gleichschaltung* (1933–4)

1933
30 January: Hitler appointed Chancellor in mixed cabinet
5 March: elections – NSDAP poll 43.9% of vote
23 March: Enabling Act
2 May: Abolition of trade unions
14 July: Law against the Formation of New Parties

1934
30 January: formal abolition of political devolution in federal states (Länder)
30 June – 2 July: 'Röhm putsch' or 'Night of the Long Knives'
Hitler combines roles of Chancellor and President as Führer following death of
        Hindenburg on 2 August; Army swears oath of allegiance to Hitler

Phase II: A 'dual state' (1934–8)

1935
13 January: Saar plebiscite; Saar returns to Reich in March
September: 'Nuremberg Laws' announced at NSDAP Party Conference

1936
Army marches into demilitarised Rhineland
'Four Year Plan' announced, with Goering in charge

1937
November: 'Hossbach memorandum' – Hitler announces ambitious war plans

Phase III: 'Radicalisation' (1938–45)

1938
February: Army leadership purged and 'nazified'
March: *Anschluss* of Austria
September: 'Munich Agreement' averts war by ceding Czech Sudetenland to Reich
Radicalisation of anti-Semitic policies

1939
September: outbreak of war following German invasion of Poland

1941
December: Invasion of USSR in June, declaration of war on USA

1942
Wannsee Conference – coordinates 'Final Solution of the Jewish Question'

1945
Suicide of Hitler and military defeat of Germany

THE question of whether Hitler was a 'weak dictator' matters massively. Answers to this question have not been purely academic, but have been of enormous personal and political significance. The debates have taken many forms over the last sixty years, but underlying all the twists and turns of the historical controversies lies a common moral thread. A 'strong dictator' capable of realising his intentions and imposing his own will would leave little space for alternatives. On the other hand, if Hitler were a 'weak dictator', far wider circles would be implicated in questions of guilt and complicity. Debates over whether Hitler was a 'weak dictator' are thus tangled up with wider debates over collaboration and opposition, racial policy and foreign policy. In short, the question of how to evaluate Hitler's role as dictator is central to understanding the Third Reich.

Some historical controversies concern specific hypotheses which can be resolved by further empirical research and new evidence. Other historical controversies are harder to resolve because they hinge on completely different interpretations of what is essentially the same evidence. This is the case in relation to many aspects of the debates over Hitler's role in the Nazi state.

The development of the historical debates

Debates over Hitler's role began already during the Third Reich. Much of Nazi propaganda was devoted to portraying the regime as a streamlined state, with a pyramid of power culminating in the figure of the *Führer* at its peak. Yet some contemporary observers recognised that the structures of power in the Third Reich were not quite this simple, and the 'duality' of the old state structures which continued to operate alongside new Party organisations led Ernst Fraenkel, for example, to develop notions of a '*Dual State*' (1941), while Franz Neumann presented the image of a many-headed monster in his *Behemoth* (1942).

Totalitarian theories in the 1950s and 1960s

In the immediate post-war period, however, the focus on Hitler himself remained predominant. Presented as a positive image while Hitler was in power, Hitler's supremacy was simply given a negative shading after 1945. For many Germans agonising over their recent past, condemnation of Hitler as a kind of magician who had blinded the masses with his charisma and led innocent Germans astray was highly appealing. It seemed both to exonerate them from blame, and to account for Hitler's undoubted mass appeal. So too did a focus on power and oppression, and the notion that there was no alternative to carrying out *Führer-Befehl* ('Hitler's orders').

The older notion of totalitarianism was revived in the 1950s and 1960s. In Hannah Arendt's use of this term in her seminal analysis of *The Origins of Totalitarianism* (1951), the emphasis was on the dynamism of the movement, and on the mobilisation of the masses by a demonic leader, drawing attention to dictatorships of left and right, Nazism and Stalinism. The similarities between fascist and Communist dictatorships were identified rather differently in the work of Friedrich and Brzezinski (1956), who defined totalitarianism in terms of a formal list of attributes: a state with one party and one official ideology, capable of dominating the population through a monopoly of the means of propaganda (the media) and coercion (police and army) as well as control of the economy. Later critics of the concept were quick to note that these definitions were very different from one another, leading to quite different conclusions about whether Nazism or Stalinism was 'more' or 'less' totalitarian; but as a label of political critique, making a sharp distinction between democracy and dictatorship, the term had its uses.

The effective equation of Nazism and Communism under the more general concept of totalitarianism was politically convenient as a 'bridging' ideology in the West in the Cold War. (Meanwhile, in Communist East Germany a rather different notion of Nazism as a form of fascism rooted in **monopoly capitalism** was being developed; this too, by shifting blame to the 'capitalist-imperialists' and large land-owning classes, managed conveniently to exonerate the allegedly innocent German 'workers and peasants' from any blame.) According to widely held views in West Germany, many crimes had been perpetrated 'in the name of the Germans' – who allegedly had 'known nothing about it' – by 'Hitler and his henchmen'. A focus on Hitler as the almost archetypal 'strong dictator' has pervaded images of Hitler ever since, present in innumerable popular films and documentaries, as well as presenting a continuing thread in the historiography.

The emergence of notions of Hitler as 'weak dictator'

Yet, particularly from the later 1960s onwards, Western historians began to register increasing unease about this representation of Hitler's role. Historians providing evidence for the war crimes trials of the 1960s, including the famous **Auschwitz** trial, began to realise that the system of terror was not sustained by 'Hitler's orders' alone

Monopoly capitalism: A phrase used by Marxists for a particular stage of advanced capitalism, in which capital is increasingly concentrated in fewer and fewer hands.

Auschwitz: The largest of the Nazi concentration camps, including the infamous extermination centre at Auschwitz-Birkenau, as well as Auschwitz I, where Josef Mengele carried out his notorious 'medical' experiments, and subsidiary camps where slave labourers were worked to death for major German industrial enterprises. At the height of the killings in the summer of 1944, over 9000 people could be killed within 24 hours in the gas chambers of Auschwitz.

(Buchheim et al., *Anatomy of the SS – State* (1967)). A number of studies began to demonstrate that the structures of power in the Third Reich were far more complex than had previously been realised.

The notion of Hitler as strong dictator was explicitly challenged by Edward N. Peterson in his path-breaking book, *The Limits of Hitler's Power* (1969). In this detailed exploration of central and regional government, Peterson painted a picture of confusion, competition and rivalry. There were rivalries not merely between the old state apparatus and the new party institutions, but also splits and tensions within each of these, and cross-cutting tensions with and within other groups such as the Army and different sections of big business. In effect, Peterson's work amounted to a revolution in conceptions of Hitler: far from being the strong dictator of official imagery and popular imagination, Hitler was in fact a weak dictator.

The debate between structuralists (functionalists) and intentionalists

Hans Mommsen, who first started developing the notion of weak dictator in his 1960s work on civil servants in the Third Reich, also emphasised Hitler's personal insecurity, his unwillingness to take decisions, his over-dependence on popularity and willingness to agree with the last powerful person who had talked to him. Historians such as Martin Broszat began to explore the complex, ever more chaotic structures of power, in what they termed a 'polycratic state' – a state with multiple, competing and overlapping, centres of power (see **Landmark Study** below). This became known as the 'structuralist' approach, in which the explanatory focus was shifted to the ways the institutional structure functioned; hence, it is also sometimes termed a 'functionalist' interpretation.

Such an approach contrasts strongly with the interpretation presented by those who emphasise Hitler's intentions and 'world view' (as explored by Eberhard Jaeckel in his book *Hitler's*

Landmark Study   The book that changed people's views

Martin Broszat, *The Hitler State* (Longman, 1969)

In his seminal analysis of the 'Hitler state', Broszat argued that the 'proliferation of arbitrary decisions and acts of violence' could not be explained by changes in Hitler's personality. Rather, he suggested, 'we can only explain why the Hitler regime ultimately fell prey to a policy of irrational self-destruction after years of astonishingly impressive success, against the background of ever-changing structural and institutional circumstances'. Thus the causal focus should be on the structures of power, and not on the individual personality of Hitler.

Weltanschauung: A Blueprint for Power, 1972). In Karl Dietrich Bracher's detailed analysis (*The German Dictatorship*, 1969) Hitler's 'programme' and ultimate goals presented the driving force in what – despite Bracher's recognition of conflicts among different power groups – remained for Bracher essentially a 'totalitarian' state. For 'Hitler-centric' historians such as Andreas Hillgruber or Klaus Hildebrand (*The Third Reich*, 1984), the policies of world conquest and racial extermination must be explained primarily in terms of Hitler's intentions. For intentionalist historians, then, Hitler remains a strong dictator.

These controversies between structuralists and intentionalists were analysed in a key contribution by Tim Mason at a conference in 1979, where the political and moral implications of different historical interpretations gave rise to a particularly heated debate. This controversy exploded in the 1980s into an extended debate on the origins of the Holocaust. There are a number of ways of evaluating these conflicting interpretations, including: changing structures of power; Hitler's leadership style; and the implementation of policies.

How did political structures develop in the process of 'cumulative radicalisation'?

The real 'seizure of power'? *Gleichschaltung* or co-ordination (1933–4)

The first 18 months of Hitler's rule saw the ruthless establishment of a dictatorial one-party state. This involved the systematic dismantling of the liberal-democratic constitution, the destruction of **federalism** and the imposition of Nazi rule in the localities, and the destruction of the organisational bases for political opposition, independent association and freedom of speech. The real *Machtergreifung* ('seizure of power') after his constitutional appointment as Chancellor does indeed initially seem to lend support to the view of Hitler as strong dictator.

Federalism: A devolved system of government in a federal state with considerable regional powers.

Despite the political capital the Nazis made out of the Reichstag Fire of 27 February, using it to declare a state of emergency and to persecute Communists and socialists, the NSDAP failed to gain an absolute majority in the Election of 5 March 1933, polling just under 44 per cent of the vote. Nevertheless, the Enabling Act of March 1933 (the necessary two-thirds majority having been cobbled together by a combination of coercion and persuasion) allowed Hitler to change the constitution at will and to pass any legislation he wanted.

The first concentration camp for political opponents, Dachau, was opened in March. The 'Law for the Restoration of a Professional Civil Service' of April 1933 purged the professions of Jews, socialists and other potential opponents of the regime. The dismantling of local government autonomy also began with the imposition of *Reichsstatthalter* ('Reich Governors') in the *Länder* ('provinces') in the spring of 1933, and was finalised with a 'Law for the Reconstruction of the Reich' abolishing their constitutional role in January 1934. After the celebration of the traditional day of labour on 1 May 1933, on 2 May independent trade unions were abolished and labour was rapidly incorporated in Robert Ley's 'German Labour Front' (DAF). Following the ban on the Social Democratic Party in June, the other political parties dissolved themselves, and the role of the NSDAP as the only legally permitted party was enshrined in the 'Law against the Formation of New Parties' of 14 July 1933. Within six months of coming to power, Hitler appeared to have control not only over the political system and the means of coercion, but also over many aspects of social and cultural life.

The first stage of the construction of the dictatorship culminated in August 1934. Following President Hindenburg's death on 2 August, Hitler combined the roles of President and Chancellor into that of *Führer*, thus uniting the roles of head of state and head of government. In light of the beheading of the SA, including its leader, Ernst Röhm, in the **Night of the Long Knives** a month earlier, the Army swore a personal oath of allegiance to Hitler.

Night of the Long Knives: The killing on 30 June 1934 (continuing until 1 July) of senior members of the SA, including its leader Ernst Röhm, and other potential political rivals of Hitler. The total number murdered was somewhere between 85 and 200 people.

All of this makes it look like a simple case of a single-party state in which the leader of the party, Adolf Hitler, held absolute power – although, it should be noted, power sustained by compromising some of his own party's more radical interests with those of traditional authorities such as the Army. Yet – as just indicated – the realities were rather more complex. Since Hitler had come to power entirely by legal, constitutional means, he inherited the structures of a modern bureaucratic state. There was, moreover, much in this system which was essential for the running of an advanced industrial economy, and most importantly, for the preparation for war. Thus Hitler had to reach certain compromises with key traditional elites – particularly conservative nationalists in the civil service and the Army – and with powerful economic interests in order to pursue his ultimate, overriding objectives.

An unstable 'congruence of aims'? The 'dual state' (1934–7)

In the apparently 'stable' middle years, such compromises worked – but only up to a point. While the Army and the conservative nationalists had a real interest in rearmament and revision of the Treaty of Versailles, and industrialists had an interest in the suppression of the rights of labour and the return to a stable economy, there were other elements in this rather volatile equation.

On the one hand, there was repeated pressure from party activists for radical change, dynamism, continual revolution – an echo, particularly among older party members, of the pre-1933 dynamism of the party as a mobilising force. There was at the same time the continual concern of Hitler himself with his own image and popularity among the majority of the German people, requiring him to keep a constant eye on public opinion. He had no wish to be associated with the less popular actions of, for example, the Nazi *Gauleiter* in the provinces, or with unpopular policy decisions on particular issues which affected people's day-to-day lives. Hitler's key policies remained vague and essentially negative: to rid Germany of a range of 'community aliens' (defined in racist and biological terms), to attack socialists and Communists, to acquire 'living space' and make Germany great again on the international stage. He had little interest in the nitty-gritty of the day-to-day details of running a modern state and economy. Such a combination was hardly likely to produce stability for long.

Gauleiter. Nazi Party officials at regional and district level, who could build up considerable local power bases.

In the event, what developed was a curious hybrid: an ever-changing set of Nazi party institutions and practices was superimposed on old bureaucratic administrative structures, creating growing complexity and rivalry between party and state organisations. There were personal rivalries within the party, with its essentially feudal structures, personal loyalties and individual fiefdoms. Similar rivalries were increasingly characteristic of civil service organisations too. Given Hitler's distrust of ministers meeting to confer informally with one another – the only way they could even seek to coordinate policies, as normal practices of cabinet government were discontinued – there was a lack of cooperation among the state ministries, and a lack of coordination of policy. Competition and rivalry was further exacerbated by the creation of new, hybrid institutions, and by Hitler's habit of appointing 'plenipotentiaries' (people with an almost unlimited and ill-defined brief) for particular purposes. All this seemed to lead to 'government without administration', in many respects without direction, apparently out of control.

**Heinrich Himmler
(1900–45)**

After a stint in chicken farming, Himmler, who had participated in the 1923 Beer Hall Putsch, was appointed head of Hitler's personal bodyguard, the SS (*Schutzstaffel*), in January 1929, which at that time numbered only 200 men. Himmler organised the purge of 30 June 1934 which beheaded the SA, and built up the SS, which had initially been subordinated to the SA, to become the key instrument of terror in the Nazi state. In 1936 Himmler became 'Reichsführer SS and Chief of the German Police in the Ministry of the Interior', thus controlling both the regular police force and the security police. During the war, he controlled a veritable empire of power through the 'Reich Security Main Office' (RSHA), the criminal police and the Gestapo, as well as the various sections of the SS and Waffen-SS; and he oversaw and masterminded the 'Final Solution of the Jewish Question' with a combination of misplaced idealism and racist brutality. On being arrested by the British at the end of the war, Himmler committed suicide with a poison pill.

Often Nazi institutions competed with state institutions over the same ground: for example, Goebbels' empire controlling 'Propaganda and Enlightenment' challenged the state's responsibility for Science, Education and Popular Education; while Robert Ley's German Labour Front (DAF) sought to outweigh the Ministry of Labour. In other cases, aspects of pre-1933 Nazi ideology were abandoned in favour of other goals, as with conflicting demands for social revolution and the economic needs of rearmament (discussed in the next chapter), creating further rivalries. Powerful personal empires could be built up through combinations of party and state offices, as in 1936 when **Heinrich Himmler** was appointed '*Reichsführer* SS and Chief of the German Police in the Ministry of the Interior', controlling both the regular police force and the security police (under **Reinhard Heydrich**).

**Reinhard Heydrich
(1904–42)**
In July 1931, after being forced to resign from the Navy for misconduct,

Heydrich joined the NSDAP and then the SS. Tall, blond and blue-eyed, he soon became Himmler's right-hand man, and from 1936 controlled the security police in the Reich. A master of intrigue, Heydrich engineered the downfall of von Blomberg and von Fritsch in 1938, and provided the pretext for Hitler's invasion of Poland in September 1939 which started the Second World War. He became head of the RSHA in 1939, thus controlling the Gestapo, the criminal police and the SD. Heydrich played a major role in the 'Final Solution of the Jewish Question', directing the *Einsatzgruppen* who carried out mass killings in the Soviet Union in 1941, and convening the 'Wannsee Conference' of January 1942 to coordinate the implementation of genocide. He became Deputy Reich Protector of Bohemia and Moravia in September 1941, and died on 4 June 1942 following an attack by two members of the Czech Resistance. His assassination was hideously avenged by complete destruction of the village of Lidice where it occurred and estimates of perhaps 1300 to 4000 related murders.

'Cumulative radicalisation'? 1938–45

This essentially unstable situation tipped over into a more radical phase in the winter of 1937–8. Following Hitler's lengthy speech in November 1937 to the Army leadership outlining megalomaniac plans for eventual world domination – a speech captured in the 'memorandum' penned by one of those present, Hossbach – increasing disquiet was registered by military leaders. In the spring of 1938, control over military matters and foreign affairs was distinctly 'Nazified': the War Minister, Werner von Blomberg, and the Commander-in-Chief of the Army, Werner von Fritsch, were dismissed (involving personal scandals and smears on the private lives of each). Following some institutional reorganisation, they were replaced by Generals Wilhelm Keitel and Walther von Brauchitsch; Foreign Minister Konstantin von Neurath resigned and was replaced by Joachim von Ribbentrop; and Hitler himself took over general command of the Army. In 1938–9 the regime entered a distinctly more radical phase in both foreign and racial policies, including: the annexation of Austria in the *Anschluss* of March 1938; the Sudeten crisis culminating in the Munich Agreement of September 1938; and the stepping-up of discrimination and violence against Jews, the seizure of Jewish property and businesses, pressures for emigration, and the pogrom known as the **Reichskristallnacht** of 9 November 1938.

The process of radicalisation became ever more apparent after the German invasion of Poland in September 1939 provoked war in Europe. Hitler's personal control of military strategy could, with luck, produce breathtaking successes, as in the *Blitzkrieg* of the early months; but in the longer term his ideologically driven decisions were suicidal. The unprecedented brutality following the invasion of the Soviet Union in June 1941, the hubris of declaration of war on the USA following the Japanese attack on Pearl Harbor in December 1941, the unleashing of the murderous **'Final Solution of the Jewish Question'** – all these raise fundamental questions as to the role of Hitler's own intentions in what has variously been described as the 'twisted road to Auschwitz' and the 'German catastrophe'

Reichskristallnacht: Literally, 'crystal night': a night of organised violence against Jewish property, including arson attacks on synagogues and the smashing of windows in Jewish department stores, followed by the arrests and imprisonment of many Jews and the demand that they foot the bill for the damage caused.

'Final solution of the Jewish question': The Nazi euphemism for the Holocaust: the fact that, in order to 'remove' Jews from Europe, Jews were being systematically murdered in very large numbers.

Does Hitler's leadership style provide evidence of strength or weakness?

Images of power

What then was Hitler's own role in this changing situation? At first glance, Hitler's style of leadership appears almost self-evidently to be that of a strong dictator. His own position within the party was unique, even in the 1920s: from his re-entry into politics in 1925 onwards, he embodied the **Movement**, and his 'Will' was frequently decisive. Once in power, the appearance of strength was massively reinforced. The presentation of Hitler's image in Nazi propaganda, such as **Leni Riefenstahl's** film of the 1934 Nuremberg Party Rally, *Triumph of the Will*, is that of the supreme dictator, capable of uniting the *Volk*, attracting the adulation of the masses, and confidently leading the German people towards their glorious destiny as 'master race'. Hitler appeared personally to embody the slogan *'Ein Volk, ein Reich, ein Führer!'* ('One People, one Empire, one Leader!').

The orchestration of ceremonial displays of power – serried ranks of the SA or the SS, the Hitler Youth organisation (*Hitler Jugend*) or the League of German Maidens (*Bund deutscher Mädel*) – added to the image of a well-organised, stream-lined state with Hitler at its head. So too, in a very different way, did state-sponsored terror and violence right from the outset in 1933: the rounding-up and incarceration of Communists and socialists, the exclusion of Jews and political opponents from professional occupations, the enforced sterilisation of those thought to carry hereditary diseases, the suppression of independent organisations and civil rights. It is little wonder that an image of Hitler as 'strong dictator' was readily associated with a murderous regime in which, in the six peace-time years alone, as many as 12 000 Germans were convicted of high treason.

Movement: Emphasised the dynamism of the Nazi party in contrast to other parties at this time; Hitler's image was projected as that of the saviour who would lift Germany out of the abyss.

Leni Riefenstahl (1902–2003): Film-maker, photographer and actress. Best known for her propaganda films.

Hitler's lifestyle and the practice of government

Yet on closer inspection, the realities appear more complex. Hitler had little interest in or patience with the details of policy or the bureaucratic processes of modern government. Once the Enabling Act was passed in March 1933, there was no longer any need either for parliamentary support in the Reichstag or a presidential decree for any legislation to be approved. While Hindenburg was still alive, Hitler made some effort to go through the motions of 'normal government'; he held as many as 72 formal meetings of the cabinet

Nuremberg Nazi Party rally, September 1936. These formal displays of power created an image of a powerful and well-ordered state with Hitler at its head.

in 1933. But by 1937 the number of cabinet meetings had declined to a mere six; in 1938 there was only one such meeting, which turned out to be its last.

Hitler's own lifestyle added to the problems of efficient government: he tended to rise late, and enjoyed watching films, talking with friends, indulging in architectural planning and dreaming. He disliked the German capital, Berlin, and preferred to spend as much time as possible in his Bavarian mountain retreat at Obersalzburg, with its spectacular views across the breathtaking Alpine landscape above Berchtesgaden. Thus the routine business of government was left largely to others, often having to operate without much clear guidance on specifics.

Hitler had a contempt for the life of minor officials and civil servants (harking right back to his contempt for his own father's aspirations for him which he had rejected as a young man); he had a low regard for the law, and preferred giving oral rather than written commands. He tended to side with the last person he had spoken to, and also greatly disliked taking decisions on particular policy issues. These habits often gave rise to considerable confusion, and well-founded debates between those charged with the formation and execution of contradictory policies. Hitler then often left his underlings to fight it out among themselves, taking the view – perhaps rooted in social Darwinist notions of the 'survival of the fittest' – that the strongest would inevitably win. Routine access to Hitler became ever less possible, such that eventually whoever was fortunate enough to be able to 'catch his ear' – particularly if Hitler happened to be in a good mood at the time – and could gain Hitler's personal approval for a particular proposal was able to come out claiming it was 'Hitler's will'.

Interpretations of Hitler's leadership style in political context

How then is one to interpret this leadership style? Those who argue that Hitler was a strong dictator suggest that rivalry among underlings is evidence of a policy of divide and rule. People were ultimately dependent on Hitler's personal approval for realising their plans; they had no independent institutional basis for authority, other than Hitler's will. Thus Hitler's intentions alone were decisive. When he did not get what he wanted from one quarter, he would simply instruct someone else to carry out his orders.

Those who see Hitler rather as a weak dictator have a different interpretation. They agree that, if Hitler failed to get his way by one institutional channel, he had a tendency simply to set up a rival organisation, or appoint an ad hoc 'plenipotentiary' to deal with that particular area of policy. But in Hans Mommsen's view, this meant that Hitler was ultimately a weak dictator, at the mercy of those below. Some individuals, such as **Hermann Goering** or Heinrich Himmler, were able to build up immense personal power bases;

Hermann Goering (1893–1946)
At ease in high society and fond of a luxurious life-style replete with traditional hunting pastimes and costumes to match, Goering – who had joined the NSDAP and the SA in 1922, and had taken part in the Beer Hall Putsch of 1923 – facilitated Hitler's acceptance by conservative and business elites in the later Weimar years. Alongside other offices, Goering became Prussian Minister of the Interior following Hitler's appointment as Chancellor in 1933. He collaborated with Himmler and Heydrich in setting up the network of concentration camps and terror in the Third Reich, playing a key role in exploiting the Reichstag Fire of February 1933, the Night of the Long Knives against the SA in June 1934, and the maltreatment of Jews after *Kristallnacht* in 1938. In 1936, Goering was appointed to take charge of the 'Four Year Plan Office' preparing Germany for war within four years. His increasingly powerful industrial empire brought him personally large profits. In control of the *Luftwaffe* (Air Force) during the Second World War, Goering mismanaged the attack on Britain, and began to lose Hitler's favour. Sentenced to death by hanging following the Nuremberg trial, Goering managed to commit suicide by taking a poison capsule.

others argued their corners far less successfully, but were engaged in a constant struggle for position. Hitler's hesitance in reaching decisions, and his tendency to wait to side with whoever was emerging as a winner, meant – on this view – that he was often more of a final rubber stamp than the person in the driving seat.

Recently historians have sought to combine a renewed focus on Hitler's own power with a recognition of the complexity of power structures which the structuralists rightly identified. Ian Kershaw, in a series of seminal works, suggests that Hitler's position as 'charismatic leader' was, paradoxically, in large part a product of the increasingly chaotic structures of power. With the competing, overlapping centres of power there was simply no other ultimate source of decision-making, and the 'Hitler order' was the only final authority that could be cited. Moreover, Hitler had a constant eye on his popularity with the population at large, and thus consciously sought to distance himself from day-to-day decision-making processes. At the same time, the notion of 'working towards the *Führer*' (a phrase taken from a contemporary source) encapsulates the way in which Hitler's undoubted personal power and extraordinary hold over his close followers stimulated actions 'from below' that did not always require specific orders from above. Thus, in Kershaw's interpretation, Hitler's own prejudices set the tone and ultimate aims of the regime, while underlings competed for his favour. It is possible in this way to synthesise the notion of the polycratic state, riddled by internal rivalries, with that of Hitler's supreme role at the centre, shaping the parameters and ultimate goals of the regime.

How far can policies be explained in terms of Hitler's 'programme'?

It is easy enough to write the history of the Third Reich in terms of Hitler's 'world view', expounded in virulent form as early as *Mein Kampf*. On the intentionalist view, once in power Hitler's prejudices could simply be translated into hideous reality once conditions were right. Yet on closer inspection. this seems an oversimplification. While Hitler's ultimate goals mattered more than some of the more radical proponents of the 'weak dictator' thesis might like to concede, Hitler's own intentions are merely a necessary but not a sufficient explanation of the way in which policies were actually formed and effected in the Third Reich.

Policy outcomes were always a result of a combination of different pressures and forces, the balance of which constantly

Hitler salutes a crowd of Hitler Youth members at Nuremberg.

changed. Pressures on Hitler from party radicals and activists; restraints proposed by party moderates, conservative nationalists, or civil servants; the aspirations of different economic interest groups or sections of the Army; wider public opinion, including in the peace-time years reactions abroad as well as at home – all these played a significant role in processes of policy formation. Such pressures might affect timing or details of policy – but not, where it mattered to Hitler, the overall direction and ultimate goals.

When the areas which were closest to Hitler's heart – expansionist foreign policy goals and aggressive racial policies – are examined, it is clear that Hitler never compromised in the pursuit of his ultimate aims, however much he trimmed the details of the route according to circumstances and constraints. Yet at the same time, the circles of those implicated in the realisation of these policies must be spread far wider than the intentionalist case would suggest.

Conclusion: a strong leader in a polycratic state?

The realities are more complex than either side of what has been a very polarised debate would suggest. But it now seems possible in some respects to combine aspects of both sides of the earlier debates. It seems ever more clear that the structure of the Nazi state was indeed polycratic, with many competing centres of power, and not the streamlined dictatorship suggested by the notion of totalitarianism. Yet this very complexity was in part a product of the way in which Hitler operated – appointing people to new positions, creating ad hoc posts with ill-defined powers, constantly changing the structure of the system. And, almost paradoxically, Hitler's own role as a 'charismatic leader' was itself in part a product of this increasingly chaotic power structure, since his 'will' alone remained the only decisive factor. Moreover, his undoubted wider popularity remained a key integrative factor for the regime.

Through this complex structure Hitler was in large measure able to have his own way as far as his ultimate 'negative' goals with respect to racial and foreign policy were concerned – though a devastating war of total destruction and absolute defeat hardly corresponded to Hitler's dreams of a Thousand-year Reich. To explain how such a situation developed thus implicates far wider circles, not only in the Nazi party (as in the 'Hitler and his henchmen' focus) but also in the civil service, the Army, and among the economic elites; in other words, among those who not merely helped Hitler into power in 1933 but who also thought that they could continue to negotiate compromises with Nazism in the pursuit of their own interests.

Q Was Hitler a weak dictator?

1. Read the text and answer the question.

'Everyone who has the opportunity to observe it knows that the Führer can hardly dictate from above everything which he intends to realise sooner or later. On the contrary, up till now everyone with a post in the new Germany has worked best when he has, so to speak, worked towards the Führer *... in fact it is the duty of everybody to try to work towards the* Führer *along the lines he would wish.'*

(Comment made by the Nazi Werner Willikens, State Secretary in the Reich Ministry of Agriculture, to a meeting on 21 February 1934 of representatives of state agriculture; printed in Noakes and Pridham, Vol. 2, p. 207).

In the light of this source and your own knowledge, how would you characterise Hitler's role in the Nazi system of power?

2. In what respects did the character of the Nazi state change in the period 1933–9?

3   Was there a Nazi social revolution?

What changes were there in overall social and economic structure?

Did Nazi racial policies override social class issues?

What were the effects on women, young people and culture?

Framework of events

1933	1–3 April: Boycott of Jewish shops and businesses
	7 April: 'Law for the Restoration of a Professional Civil Service'
	2 May: Abolition of trade unions – incorporated into German Labour Front (DAF)
	14 July: 'Law for the Prevention of Hereditarily Diseased Offspring'
	20 July: 'Reich Concordat' with the Pope on behalf of the Catholic Church
1935	September: 'Nuremberg Laws' announced at NSDAP Party Conference
1936	August: Summer Olympic Games in Berlin
	September: 'Four Year Plan' announced, with Goering in charge
1938	Exacerbation of wide range of measures against Jews
	November: *Reichskristallnacht* – burning of Jewish synagogues, businesses, etc.
1939	'Euthanasia' programme starts
1941	'Euthanasia' programme officially called off; mass murder of Jews begins
1942	Wannsee conference; construction of major extermination camps

'Blood and soil' ideology: *Blut und Boden*, emphasising the importance of a 'racial' community rooted in the German lands.

THE Nazis came to power proclaiming they would make a revolution – if a rather reactionary one. While in the 1920s the more radical wing of the NSDAP had taken quite seriously the words 'socialist' and 'workers' in the party name, Nazi ideology was overwhelmingly against what it considered to be the ills of 'modernity'. The **'blood and soil' ideology** presented a myth of a rural idyll, with images of strong blond peasants silhouetted against a backdrop of fruitful fields and gentle hills, in contrast to the cultural decadence and crass cosmopolitanism of modern city life. But Hitler also argued that, to achieve this pastoral paradise, the

German Labour Front propaganda poster, 1934, illustrating the 'blood and soil' ideology of the Nazi party, which emphasised a link between race and the right to live and work on the land.

German people required space, or *Lebensraum*; and that in turn meant war, which, in an industrial age, meant the use of industrial means. Hitler himself had already begun to distinguish between 'good' and 'bad' ('Jewish') aspects of capitalism well before his rise to power; and the 'nationalist' and 'German' elements in the party name for him took priority. The character of what the Nazi 'revolution' would entail in practice was therefore self-contradictory from the outset.

What is meant by 'social revolution'?

The word 'revolution' – at least in its modern non-cyclical usage – denotes rapid, fundamental, and possibly irreversible change. Most people would agree on what it takes to call something a *political* revolution, with a complete change in the character and ideology of the regime, and not merely a change in ruling personnel. But it is not so easy to agree on what constitutes a *social* revolution.

Nor is it always easy to disentangle the causes of specific observable social changes. Were particular changes the direct effects of Nazi policies, or the unintended consequences of conflicting policies and priorities? Were these changes simply further developments in pre-existing long-term trends, or the associated effects of other events? Thus, even if there were sufficiently far-reaching changes to amount to a 'social revolution', it might not be a specifically 'Nazi' social revolution.

Landmark Study The book that changed people's views

David Schoenbaum, *Hitler's Social Revolution: Class and Status in Nazi Germany 1933–1939* (Weidenfeld & Nicholson, 1966)

In this path-breaking work, David Schoenbaum explored the extent to which the social aims proclaimed by the Nazi party before 1933 were realised in practice in the Third Reich. According to Schoenbaum, class conflict continued: 'Beneath the cover of Nazi ideology, the historic social groups continued their conflicts like men wrestling under a blanket.' Thus there was no social revolution in reality. But the new opportunities provided by Nazi rule turned all traditional conceptions of status on their heads, and introduced new complexities: 'in the wonderland of Hitler Germany ... there were no longer reliable indications of what was up and what was down'. In the end, perception changed more than reality; the classless 'people's community' was not achieved and 'German society was finally united only in a negative community of fear, sacrifice and ruin'.

There were two ground-breaking works on this question, published within a year of each other in the mid-1960s. One was Ralph Dahrendorf's *Society and Democracy in Germany* (1965). Dahrendorf argued that, for all the evils that Hitler's regime unleashed on the world, it at least served to remove what Dahrendorf considered to be 'obstacles to modernisation' in German society; and, by its very destruction of traditional elites and inherited statuses, Nazism created the preconditions for the post-war democratisation of Germany.

The other classic text was David Schoenbaum's *Hitler's Social Revolution* (see **Landmark Study**, above). Starting from the Nazis' own claims about the ways in which they would transform society, Schoenbaum argued that the Nazi regime merely served to exacerbate previous trends in social and economic structure: industrialisation and urbanisation proceeded apace, reinforced by Hitler's emphasis on rearmament. For Schoenbaum, however, there were new avenues of social mobility through the Nazi party; traditional ideas of social status were challenged and overlain; popular mentalities did change; thus the 'revolution' was one in perception, not reality.

These two books stimulated an enormous amount of productive research on changes in the position of different social groups and classes, and in perceptions and patterns of collective mentality.

What changes were there in overall social and economic structure?

If 'social revolution' is defined as a radical change in overall social and economic structure, then the simple answer is that there was no Nazi social revolution. 'Modern' means were indispensable to Hitler's military goals: foreign policy took priority over vaguely defined economic and social views.

Against 'modernity' by modern means? Rearmament, industry and 'modernisation'

Hitler's determination to engage in an aggressive war of territorial expansion meant that the rearmament programme was started already in 1933; even early 'works creation schemes', such as the building of autobahns, were important in creating the infrastructure for mobilisation for war. By 1936, Hitler was determined to be ready for war 'within four years'. But this was not to be at the expense of popular support, a factor of enormous importance to Hitler as 'charismatic leader'. Faced with the choice between importing foodstuffs and importing the raw materials necessary for armaments production, Hitler insisted on both 'guns *and* butter'. When the Minister of Economics, Hjalmar Schacht, told Hitler that it was impossible to square the economic circle, Hitler simply created an ad hoc new 'Four Year Plan Office' with Goering in charge: a classic instance of the 'polycratic' system discussed in the previous chapter. In the view of some historians this meant that a successful war of conquest within four years would be essential, because this policy would be economically unsustainable in the longer run.

The effect was to favour certain sections of industry over others. The drive for self-sufficiency, or 'autarchy', favoured enterprises engaged in the production of synthetic materials, as well as those closely associated with Goering's industrial empire which received preferential treatment in the distribution of raw materials. Some made massive profits out of the Third Reich, such as the giant chemicals company I. G. Farben (which played a particularly compromised role in its exploitation of slave labour in its works at Auschwitz, even manufacturing the lethal *Zyklon B* gas used in the gas chambers). Other sections of industry – particularly those oriented to exports – benefited less from, or were even disadvantaged by, Nazi economic policies. Yet overall, the Third Reich was good for big business.

A further area which has recently received considerable attention is that of certain professional groups, such as those involved in the development of social policy, in population planning and land use, and in medical treatment and research, who cooperated very closely with the Nazi regime. Recent claims that these varied (and in their consequences utterly inhumane) professional activities provide

All of these measures radically altered the character of society in Nazi Germany: racism cross-cut social class divisions; racial policies and ideology affected all aspects of life (and death); Nazi racial categories and biological conceptions were internalised as 'natural' by many Germans. To ignore the sheer extent and implications of Nazi racism for every area of German society is to miss what was arguably the most fundamental aspect of any conceivable 'Nazi social revolution'.

What were the effects on women, young people and culture?

The effects on women's roles

The experiences of women varied dramatically according to race and politics. Here, as in so many areas of the Third Reich, rhetoric and reality were often self-contradictory. Hitler's views on women, which now appear extraordinarily sexist, were at the time fairly representative. In the Weimar period, women themselves had not voted in significant numbers for parties favouring women's emancipation; many had criticised married women who worked, as 'double earners' in a period of mass unemployment; and women's control over reproduction (contraception, abortion) remained highly controversial. Nazi ideology stressed that the role of women was in the domestic and nurturing spheres of *Kinder, Küche, Kirche* ('children, kitchen, church'). But additionally, Nazi ideology stressed the responsibility of women to the wider 'folk community', present and future.

Biological essentialism: The belief that the different roles of men and women are fundamentally rooted in biology rather than being a result of culture, upbringing, social environment and so on.

Hitler's view was one of **biological essentialism**: men and women were conceived of as fundamentally different. Hitler adopted the view of 'separate but equal' spheres, or, 'complementary worlds':

If the man's world is said to be the State, his struggle, his readiness to devote his powers to the service of the community, then it may perhaps be said that the woman's is a smaller world. For her world is her husband, her family, her children, and her home … [The] great world cannot survive if the smaller world is not stable … The two worlds are not antagonistic. They complement each other, they belong together just as man and woman belong together …

(from a speech delivered to the NSF in 1934, reprinted in Noakes and Pridham, vol.2, p.449)

The role of the 'small world' was thus to support, sustain, and reproduce the 'great world'; the purpose of the family was the reproduction of the 'master race', as in the pro-birth slogan 'every year, every woman, [should produce] a child for the *Führer*'.

In 1933, there were pressures to exclude women from jobs in teaching, the civil service, politics and law; but these were not consistently carried through. From around 1936–7, with the push for rearmament and growing shortage of labour, anti-feminist ideology and the demands of economy were increasingly mutually contradictory. While in 1933, 34.4 per cent of women worked, by 1939 this had risen to 36.7 per cent. Moreover, women's occupational roles became ever more visible: increasing numbers were employed in trade, industry, service and government, with a decline in the proportion employed in less visible roles as domestic servants. The number of married women working rose by two million. During the war, there were conflicts in the Nazi hierarchy between those who sought to use women in the labour force, and those who continued to prioritise the domestic ideology of reproduction. Similarly, despite Nazi views, many women were able to take up vacant university places when men were away at the front.

The *Deutsches Frauenwerk* (*DFW*) was an umbrella organisation subsuming former middle-class women's organisations, with around 1.8 million members; the *NS Frauenschaft* (*NSF*) was the specifically Nazi women's organisation with around 2.3 million members by 1938. Many women gained experience of leadership roles in these organisations, and in the Nazi girls' movement, the *Bund deutscher Mädel* (*BdM*). But, as Jill Stephenson (*Women in Nazi Germany*, 2001) points out, such experience was in areas without much wider political influence.

Those considered to be 'healthy breeding stock' were encouraged to produce as many 'racially desirable' children as possible. There were tax incentives, subsidies, housing loans and 'Mother's crosses' – a bronze cross for four children, silver for six, and gold for eight. The use of contraception was prohibited, and Paragraph 218 of the Civil Code outlawing abortion was rigorously enforced, with fierce penalties for infringement. An ideology of German motherhood was actively fostered: the *Deutsches Frauenwerk* organised 'Mothers' Schools' and there was a 'Mother and Child' organisation in the *NSV* (Nazi welfare organisation). *Lebensborn* institutions would care for pregnant women of 'healthy stock' irrespective of marital status.

There was an overall rise in births, from a low of 14.7 per thousand in 1933 to a high of 20.3 per thousand in 1939. But this rise was not necessarily a direct effect of Nazi policies; it can be explained in terms evidence of a Nazi contribution to a long-term 'modernisation' of 20th-century German society are however highly controversial and strongly contested.

A pastoral paradise? The peasantry and lower middle classes

Neither peasants nor sections of the lower middle classes got quite what they were expecting or felt they had been promised. Peasants on the whole were rewarded with little more than the idealisation of their virtues in the 'blood and soil' ideology; they disliked measures which reduced their own autonomy and independent decision-making, such as the control of agricultural prices, production and distribution by the **Reich Food Estate**, or the restrictions placed on the division and disposal of inherited property under the **Entailed Farm Law**. With the growing shortage of skilled labour in the period of rapid rearmament after 1936, many peasants left the land in order to earn higher wages in the towns, contributing further to pre-existing tendencies to urbanisation.

Meanwhile, despite some half-hearted measures by the regime, the position of the lower middle classes was not materially improved. Big department stores continued to squeeze out small shopkeepers; small enterprises could not compete on equal terms with big business for labour and raw materials; and few other than leading Nazis benefited from the **Aryanisation of Jewish property** in 1938.

The mixed experiences of the working class

Workers had by and large not expected much from the Third Reich; the majority had remained loyal to the SPD and KPD up to 1933; significant numbers had actively opposed the Nazis. Many soon found the realities even worse than they had feared possible, with intimidation, brutal treatment and incarceration of socialists and Communists. Within a matter of months, workers were left with no independent political or trade union organisations to represent their interests. Yet the picture with respect to the German working class is a mixed one.

Many ordinary working people – at least those who were able to stay in and survive the Third Reich – later remembered the peace-time years of the Third Reich as one of the best periods of their lives. There was a return to full employment, with Hitler taking the credit for a trend that was setting in already in late 1932; by the later 1930s, there was a shortage of skilled labour. Average wages rose, though in

Reich Food Estate: A large corporate organisation created in September 1933, under the peasant leader Richard Walther Darré, to regulate the production, distribution and prices of agricultural produce in the interests of the 'economy as a whole and the common good'.

Entailed Farm Law: A law passed in September 1933 designed to strengthen the links between the people and the land and to preserve small to medium-sized farms (between 7.5 and 125 hectares) belonging to 'German citizens of German blood or similar race' by preventing sale or division, insisting they should be passed on undivided to a single heir.

Aryanisation of Jewish Property: The liquidation or forcible transfer into non-Jewish hands of Jewish businesses and shops, and the exclusion of Jews from German economic life.

part due simply to working much longer hours, and also varying according to the 'performance principle', with skilled workers benefiting more than unskilled. With profits rising even faster, the overall share of national income taken by wages actually decreased. But for many workers memories of hunger and unemployment in the Weimar period outweighed any such considerations.

Organisations and initiatives such as *Schönheit der Arbeit* ('Beauty of Labour') and *Kraft durch Freude* (*KdF*, or 'Strength through Joy') promised more in the propaganda than they delivered in practice; widely advertised cruises on the Norwegian fjords were enjoyed by only a very select group, and *KdF* holiday schemes disproportionately benefited the middle classes. But many workers nevertheless appreciated the odd day out on a factory trip to the Black Forest, or the sense of community that was fostered on a small scale by social activities and welfare measures based in their place of employment.

A classless 'people's community'?

Old status hierarchies were not destroyed, but merely overlain, by new chances for upwards mobility through Nazi organisations. A sense of a genuine 'people's community' overriding old class divisions was at best only partially achieved. Many Germans were capable of simultaneously grumbling over material measures which affected them adversely, applauding peaceful foreign policy triumphs, criticising the local Nazi big-wig, and putting all their faith in the *Führer* who, 'if only he knew', would surely set all things right. Old status distinctions were maintained. Ian Kershaw thus disagrees with Schoenbaum's view that there was at least a revolution in *perceptions*, if not social realities.

There were, too, major differences in perception between people of different ages and backgrounds. Younger generations, who had no experience of independent trade unions, had less sense of class solidarity than older workers; those who were politically committed anti-Nazis, or had strong religious and moral beliefs, were more acutely aware of deep injustices and less easily taken in by the *Führer* myth than others. It is important not to generalise about 'the Germans', or about particular social classes and their material interests, without also making such further distinctions.

An urban, industrial, 'modern' society

Nazi Germany thus remained an urbanising, class-divided industrial capitalist society. On the socio-economic definition, then, there was no social revolution. This does not, however, mean that there were no fundamental and far-reaching social changes in the 12 years of Nazi rule.

Did Nazi racial policies override social class issues?

Eugenic theories: Theories about genetics and heredity in a population. The eugenics movement of the early 20th century feared that a declining birth-rate among 'better' members of the population would eventually lead to being swamped by 'inferior' social groups who tended to have more children.

Much of the early research on social change in Nazi Germany was carried out when social class was a key concept in the minds of many historians. The growth and popularity of the social sciences in the 1960s fostered more sociological approaches to history; and, in certain circles, the revival of Marxist approaches prompted much research on working class history in particular, over which a number of historical battles were fought. But this focus arguably presents a distorted image of the most fundamental inequalities in what has been dubbed a 'racial state' (Michael Burleigh and Wolfgang Wippermann, *The Racial State*, 1991).

The 'racial' hierarchy that was built into Nazi ideology had radical implications for Nazi society long before it turned into a policy of mass murder. Quasi-biological notions, supported by Nazi 'racial science' and more widely held **eugenic theories**, were harnessed in

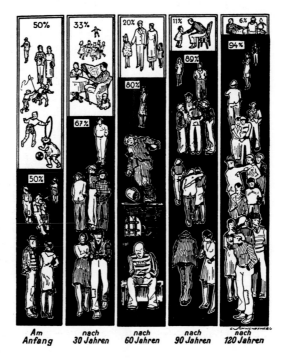

Nazi diagram showing how, in the course of four generations, the 'superior' elements of German society would be 'swamped' by the 'inferior' elements unless strict policies to increase the fertility of the former and restrict the reproduction of the latter were pursued.

service of brutal policies designed to produce a 'healthy stock' – which could only be achieved by excluding those who were 'inferior', even 'pollutants' of the 'healthy folk community'.

Already from the summer of 1933 there was compulsory sterilisation for those deemed unfit to reproduce, legitimated in the 'Law for the Prevention of Hereditarily Diseased Offspring'. Around 400 000 people were forcibly prevented from ever being able to have children by this law, on grounds ranging from ill-defined 'feeble-mindedness', through supposedly inheritable conditions such as schizophrenia, manic depression, and epilepsy, to blindness, deafness and bodily deformities; 'chronic alcoholism' was a further ground for compulsory sterilisation. People who were not considered suitable – for example those designated as 'a-socials' – were not eligible for welfare benefits. The underlying stereotyping, stigmatisation and discrimination against Germans with mental and physical disabilities, homosexuals, alcoholics and other 'a-socials', as well as those excluded on 'racial' and political grounds, formed the background to, and perhaps an essential prerequisite for, later more radical policies of euthanasia and mass murder.

From the spring of 1933 – again, legitimated in the 'Law for the Restoration for a Professional Civil Service' of April 1933 – German Jews and others were excluded from professional jobs. Many immediately lost their livelihood in areas such as the law, medicine, the universities and schools. The Nuremberg Laws of 1935 had a further impact in forbidding marriage between Jews and non-Jews, and the formal bestowal of second-class citizenship on Jews. The general introduction into everyday vocabulary of terms such as *Mischling* ('of mixed descent') introduced racial categories subtly into the minds of people who had not necessarily previously thought in this way. With the 'Aryanisation' (expropriation from Jewish ownership) of Jewish property in 1938, many Jews lost their businesses and livelihoods; they were excluded from places of enter-tainment and leisure; thousands emigrated before the start of the war. In the eight years from 1933 to 1941, additionally perhaps 35 000 non-Jewish Germans also chose to go into exile.

Meanwhile, an influx of foreign labour – which was dramatically increased in the war-time years, rising from three million in 1941 to well over seven million by 1944 – meant that racial hierarchies often overlaid class hierarchies in the workplace. By 1944, nearly one third of those working in the mining and construction industries, and one half of agricultural workers, were foreign; hence many working class Germans were able to take on supervisory functions in a position of authority over foreign labour.

All of these measures radically altered the character of society in Nazi Germany: racism cross-cut social class divisions; racial policies and ideology affected all aspects of life (and death); Nazi racial categories and biological conceptions were internalised as 'natural' by many Germans. To ignore the sheer extent and implications of Nazi racism for every area of German society is to miss what was arguably the most fundamental aspect of any conceivable 'Nazi social revolution'.

What were the effects on women, young people and culture?

The effects on women's roles

The experiences of women varied dramatically according to race and politics. Here, as in so many areas of the Third Reich, rhetoric and reality were often self-contradictory. Hitler's views on women, which now appear extraordinarily sexist, were at the time fairly representative. In the Weimar period, women themselves had not voted in significant numbers for parties favouring women's emancipation; many had criticised married women who worked, as 'double earners' in a period of mass unemployment; and women's control over reproduction (contraception, abortion) remained highly controversial. Nazi ideology stressed that the role of women was in the domestic and nurturing spheres of *Kinder, Küche, Kirche* ('children, kitchen, church'). But additionally, Nazi ideology stressed the responsibility of women to the wider 'folk community', present and future.

Biological essentialism: The belief that the different roles of men and women are fundamentally rooted in biology rather than being a result of culture, upbringing, social environment and so on.

Hitler's view was one of **biological essentialism:** men and women were conceived of as fundamentally different. Hitler adopted the view of 'separate but equal' spheres, or, 'complementary worlds':

If the man's world is said to be the State, his struggle, his readiness to devote his powers to the service of the community, then it may perhaps be said that the woman's is a smaller world. For her world is her husband, her family, her children, and her home … [The] great world cannot survive if the smaller world is not stable … The two worlds are not antagonistic. They complement each other, they belong together just as man and woman belong together …

(from a speech delivered to the NSF in 1934, reprinted in Noakes and Pridham, vol.2, p.449)

The role of the 'small world' was thus to support, sustain, and reproduce the 'great world'; the purpose of the family was the reproduction of the 'master race', as in the pro-birth slogan 'every year, every woman, [should produce] a child for the *Führer*'.

In 1933, there were pressures to exclude women from jobs in teaching, the civil service, politics and law; but these were not consistently carried through. From around 1936–7, with the push for rearmament and growing shortage of labour, anti-feminist ideology and the demands of economy were increasingly mutually contradictory. While in 1933, 34.4 per cent of women worked, by 1939 this had risen to 36.7 per cent. Moreover, women's occupational roles became ever more visible: increasing numbers were employed in trade, industry, service and government, with a decline in the proportion employed in less visible roles as domestic servants. The number of married women working rose by two million. During the war, there were conflicts in the Nazi hierarchy between those who sought to use women in the labour force, and those who continued to prioritise the domestic ideology of reproduction. Similarly, despite Nazi views, many women were able to take up vacant university places when men were away at the front.

The *Deutsches Frauenwerk* (*DFW*) was an umbrella organisation subsuming former middle-class women's organisations, with around 1.8 million members; the *NS Frauenschaft* (*NSF*) was the specifically Nazi women's organisation with around 2.3 million members by 1938. Many women gained experience of leadership roles in these organisations, and in the Nazi girls' movement, the *Bund deutscher Mädel* (*BdM*). But, as Jill Stephenson (*Women in Nazi Germany*, 2001) points out, such experience was in areas without much wider political influence.

Those considered to be 'healthy breeding stock' were encouraged to produce as many 'racially desirable' children as possible. There were tax incentives, subsidies, housing loans and 'Mother's crosses' – a bronze cross for four children, silver for six, and gold for eight. The use of contraception was prohibited, and Paragraph 218 of the Civil Code outlawing abortion was rigorously enforced, with fierce penalties for infringement. An ideology of German motherhood was actively fostered: the *Deutsches Frauenwerk* organised 'Mothers' Schools' and there was a 'Mother and Child' organisation in the *NSV* (Nazi welfare organisation). *Lebensborn* institutions would care for pregnant women of 'healthy stock' irrespective of marital status.

There was an overall rise in births, from a low of 14.7 per thousand in 1933 to a high of 20.3 per thousand in 1939. But this rise was not necessarily a direct effect of Nazi policies; it can be explained in terms of increasing confidence in conditions of economic recovery; nor did the birth rate even fully recover to pre-Depression levels. With the war came the collapse of traditional family life, but also a rise in numbers of marriages, and numbers of illegitimate children.

Women who were by contrast thought undesirable as breeders of the future master race were subjected to compulsory sterilisation; and, at the end of the spectrum, 'racially inferior' women (such as Jews and gypsies) and others who were outcastes in the Nazi world view (Jehovah's Witnesses, lesbians, political opponents) faced forced labour or murder in the death camps.

Far more important than Nazi policies themselves was the experience of life – and death – in the Third Reich. In wartime, women often became not only the chief breadwinners but also the key to a family's physical and psychological survival; they took responsibility for their children's education and discipline, for the flight to the air raid shelter at night, and for the organisation of food, water and clothing.

In the immediate post-war period, images of the so-called *Trümmerfrauen* – the 'women of the ruins' or 'rubble women' who cleared the ruins – came to stand for female strength, resilience and the determination to rebuild and return to normality. However much this image is overstated – there were many women who collapsed with malnutrition, physical exhaustion and mental breakdowns – the experience of war dramatically altered women's roles. Even the return of emaciated, often physically mutilated and psychologically damaged men-folk from Prisoner of War camps only served to underline the changed image of women. But, while women continued to work in Communist East Germany, in the post-war capitalist West women were soon encouraged to return to the home and resume more traditional roles.

It is quite clear that the record of women's experiences in the Third Reich was exceedingly variable according to class, politics and 'racial' categorisation. And the demands and experiences of war made far more of a difference than any Nazi policies or Hitler's views on women's roles.

The effects on young people

The future of the *Volk* was crucial: hence young people were a particular target for attempted influence. The official Nazi youth organisation, the *Hitler Jugend* (*HJ*, or 'Hitler Youth') became an official educational institution in 1936; membership was made compulsory in March 1939. For girls, the parallel organisation was the *Bund deutscher Mädel* (*BdM*, or 'League of German Maidens').

In schools, there was an increased emphasis on physical fitness and discipline; new subjects were introduced, such as *Rassenkunde* ('racial science'), while traditional subjects such as history, biology, German, and even maths were subverted to serve the purposes of Nazi ideology. Politically unreliable as well as 'racially inferior' teachers were purged, and special schools, such as the **Adolf-Hitler Schools** and the **NAPOLA**, were introduced as training grounds for the new Nazi elite.

What is often called the 'Hitler Youth generation' may have been particularly affected by socialisation under Nazism. But the experience of war, of bombing raids, of being thrown into combat at a tender age, the loss of fathers and elder brothers, may have had an even stronger impact on the collective character of this generation.

Adolf-Hitler Schools: Separate party-controlled schools under the *Hitler Jugend*, of which the first was founded in 1937. In total only ten were founded, with a total annual intake of 600 pupils.

NAPOLA: 'National Political Educational Institutions': state-controlled boarding schools to train a new Nazi elite, somewhat similar to the old military cadet schools. The first three were founded in 1933, and the total number had risen to 21 by 1938; they were increasingly under the influence of the SS.

Symbolic book burning of 1933: Books by Jewish and other 'undesirable' authors were thrown into a huge bonfire and burnt as a symbolic act of destruction.

Culture and mentalities

The previously independent press and media were taken over by **Goebbels**' Ministry of Propaganda and Popular Enlightenment, and their message brought into line with that portrayed by the Nazi-controlled newspaper *Völkischer Beobachter*. Leni Riefenstahl's documentaries of the 1934 Nuremberg Nazi Party Rally and the 1936 Berlin Olympics made use of innovative techniques, camera angles and artistic sophistication, to produce an image of the Third Reich which glorified Hitler's role in uniting an apparently adulatory people. Anti-Semitic films (such as *Jud Süss*) portrayed Jews as scheming, avaricious, equivalent to vermin, as did the vicious propaganda of the Nazi periodical *Der Stürmer*. The **symbolic book-burning** on 10 May 1933, and the censorship of 'Jewish' and 'degenerate' art and music, made very clear what was considered totally unacceptable. (On propaganda, see David Welch, *The Third Reich: Politics and Propaganda,* 2nd edition, 2002.)

Joseph Goebbels (1897–1945)

Hampered physically and psychologically by his club foot, small and dark-haired, Joseph Goebbels poured his intellectual energy into propaganda for the Nazi party. Initially critical of Hitler, he joined the side of the winner in 1926 and took over the Berlin section of the NSDAP; in 1929 he became Reich Propaganda Leader, and was instrumental in the NSDAP's subsequent election successes. In March 1933 Goebbels became 'Reich Minister for Public Enlightenment', with total control over the press, radio and film. He played a key role in anti-Semitic actions such as the book-burning of May 1933 and the *Kristallnacht* of November 1938, and in the ever more desperate attempts to maintain German morale in the later part of the war. He stayed with Hitler in the bunker to the last, and then, having had his six children poisoned, committed suicide alongside his wife, Magda.

With *Gleichschaltung* ('putting everything into the same gear', achieving conformity) there was a widespread take-over or abolition of independent social and cultural organisations. The one major exception was that of the Churches. The Catholic Church had come to an agreement with Hitler in the Reich Concordat of 1933, which guaranteed freedom of religious practice on condition that Catholics did not meddle in politics. The Protestant Churches split, between those *Deutsche Christen* ('German Christians') who were supportive of Hitler's attempts to co-opt the Church, and the *Bekennende Kirche* ('Confessing Church') associated with Martin Niemöller and Dietrich Bonhoeffer.

None of these attempts to control people's minds was entirely successful, as demonstrated by continued dissent and isolated acts of more active opposition. People generally had faith in Hitler as a charismatic *Führer*, rather than a belief in an anyway vague Nazi ideology. And this faith in the *Führer* collapsed as the war turned for the worse after the battle of Stalingrad; it had already more or less dissipated in many quarters even before the final defeat.

What were the effects of Hitler's rule on German society?

There were contradictions between the different demands of Nazi ideology and the economic requirements of war. The Nazi 'social

The concentration camp at Bergen-Belsen, 28 April 1945, following the arrival of British Army troops, who forced SS guards to dig graves for the masses of corpses.

revolution', as least as envisaged before 1933, therefore did not take place in either social reality or perception.

Yet Hitler's rule did serve to bring about major changes in German society. Nazi racial and foreign policies had the most fundamental effects. Millions of those excluded from Hitler's dreams were brutally murdered; others were forced to emigrate, and they – and their descendants – spread across the globe, often radically altering and enriching the characters of their new host societies as a result; many more millions were killed in warfare; and the war had profound consequences for societies across the world.

With defeat in war came – as a result of the emergent Cold War – the division of Germany, and far more fundamental and long-lasting social changes in the two successor states, which have stamped their mark on the reunified Germany of today. A continued sensitivity to the legacy of Hitler remains evident even at the start of the 21st century.

Q Was there a Nazi social revolution?

1. Read the following extract and answer the question.

    'Strength through Joy is very popular. The events appeal to the yearnings of the little man who wants an opportunity to get out and about himself and to take part in the pleasures of the "top people". It is a clever appeal to the petty bourgeois inclinations of the unpolitical workers. For such a man it really means something to have been on a trip to Scandinavia, or even if he only went to the Black Forest or the Harz Mountains, he imagines that he has thereby climbed up a rung on the social ladder ...'

    (Contemporary report by an SPD contact, Berlin, February 1938, reprinted in Noakes and Pridham, vol. 2, p.353)

    In the light of this quotation and using your own knowledge, discuss the extent to which there was (or was not) a 'social revolution' in Nazi Germany.

2. 'War, not Nazi ideology and policies, was what really changed German society.' Discuss.

Hitler: an assessment

Hitler's rise to power

Hitler did not 'seize power': he was constitutionally appointed Chancellor as a result of a unique combination of factors.

These included his own undoubted political gifts of oratory, organisation, and capacity for commanding a loyal following.

Hitler's message was only heard by large numbers of people in a time of acute economic and political crisis.

It was only because powerful elite groups also wanted to destroy democracy that the Weimar Republic eventually failed. These groups deluded themselves that they could 'tame' and make use of the upstart Hitler with his demagogic powers.

Hitler as dictator

After 1933, Hitler trod a wary line between a number of conflicting pressures from different quarters: the radical and the more moderate wings of his own party; important elites including the Army, big business, and elements of the civil service. At the same time he sought to sustain his own 'Hitler myth' and popularity among the wider populace.

This led to increasing complexity, both in the ever more chaotic structures of power, with growing rivalries among overlapping party, state and hybrid offices, and in Hitler's own curious role as charismatic leader 'above it all'.

Hitler and German society

Similarly, it meant that many aspects of the vague and often self-contradictory Nazi ideology with respect to domestic economic and social policy were never realised.

Hitler's own obsessions with racial policy and an aggressive war of expansion became ever more apparent, no longer so easily curbed by the conservative nationalists who had supported his appointment and helped to sustain him in power.

Hitler's legacy

Thus, the most enduring legacies of Hitler's rule were entirely destructive: mass genocide and World War. After 1945, the emergent Cold War between the two new superpowers inaugurated a new era in European and world history.

Further Reading

Texts specifically designed for students

Martin Broszat, *Hitler and the Collapse of Weimar Germany* Berg, 1987; original German 1984; clear analysis of factors leading to Hitler's appointment as Chancellor.

Norbert Frei, *National Socialist Rule in Germany: The Führer State, 1933–1945* Oxford: Blackwell 1993; original German 1987; includes selection of documents.

Dick Geary, *Hitler and Nazism* Routledge, 2nd edition, 2000; brief and incisive on both the rise to power and the Nazi regime.

Ian Kershaw, *The Nazi Dictatorship: Problems and Perspectives of Interpretation* Arnold, 4th edition, 2000; the ultimate guide to historical controversies, for more advanced students.

Texts for more advanced study

Pierre Ayçoberry, *The Social History of the Third Reich* The New Press, 1999; original French 1998.

Ian Kershaw, *Hitler 1889–1936: Hubris* Penguin, 1998, and *Hitler 1936–1945: Nemesis* Penguin, 2000; the currently definitive biography of Hitler. See also Ian Kershaw, *The 'Hitler Myth': Image and Reality in the Third Reich* Oxford University Press, 1987, and *Hitler: A Profile in Power* Longman, 1991

W. Laqueuer, *Fascism: A Reader's Guide* Penguin, 1979; articles by Hans Mommsen and Karl Dietrich Bracher.

John Lukacs, *The Hitler of History* Vintage Books, 1998.

Tim Mason, 'Intention and Explanation: A Current Controversy about the Interpretation of National Socialism' in G. Hirschfeld and L. Kettenacker (eds.), *The 'Führer State': Myth and Reality* Klett-Cotta, 1981; seminal article.

Jeremy Noakes and Geoffrey Pridham (eds), *Nazism* Exeter Studies in History, 1983–1998. 'The Rise to Power, 1919–1934' (vol. 1); 'State, Economy and Society, 1933–1939' (vol. 2); 'Foreign Policy, War and Racial Extermination' (vol. 3); and 'The German Home Front in World War II' (vol. 4); superb selection of documents, insightful analysis of debates.

David Schoenbaum, *Hitler's Social Revolution: Class and Status in Nazi Germany, 1933–1939* Weidenfeld and Nicolson, 1967; orig. 1966; classic text on this topic.

Jill Stephenson, *Women in Nazi Germany* Pearson, 2001; incisive and lively guide to this topic.

Index